GOA
IN DEPTH

GOA
IN DEPTH

AN A–Z GUIDE

Consulting Editor:
Louise Nicholson

Local Colour

Copyright © 1997
Local Colour Limited, Hong Kong.
All rights reserved. No part of this publication may be
produced or transmitted in any form or by any means,
electronic or mechanical, including photocopy, recording
or any information storage and retrieval system, without
permission from the publisher.

Whilst every care has been taken in compiling the text,
neither the publisher nor the author nor their respective
agents shall be responsible for any loss or damage
occasioned by any error or misleading information
contained therein or any omission therefrom.

British Library Cataloguing-in-Publication Data.
A catalogue record for this book is available from the
British Library.

Consulting Editor: Louise Nicholson
Researcher: Ralph Pereira
Maps: Uma Bhattacharya
Photography: Fredrick Arvidsson

ISBN : 962-217-388–8

Printed in Hong Kong

CONTENTS

INTRODUCTION

Goa forms a narrow strip of land, 100 kilometres long and 50 kilometres wide, on the west coast of India, approximately 400 kilometres south of Mumbai. Goa's coastline, mostly fringed by long sandy beaches, is indented by five wide estuaries into which all of Goa's five rivers flow. Eastwards, the flat coastal area gradually rises until it reaches the forested slopes of the Sahyadri mountains, part of the Western Ghats, which run from north to south. The Sahyadris also act as a natural barrier and have helped preserve Goa's distinct culture and lush setting. The tiny territory of Goa is a verdant Garden of Eden, with bottle-green hills wooded with groves of coconut, jackfruit, mango and cashewnut.

Long before the arrival of the Portuguese, the control over Goa's natural harbours was hotly contested by Hindu and Muslim princes. It was in 1498 that the Portuguese explorer, Vasco da Gama, reached the Malabar Coast. Twelve years later, a Portuguese colony was established in Goa when the greatest of Portugal's commanders, Alfonso de Albuquerque, arrived with a fresh fleet in 1510. After ten months of hard fighting he defeated the Muslims, to raise the Portuguese flag and turn Goa into a mini Portugal. Some thirty years later the ideology of the Counter Reformation arrived, importing Jesuit priests to convert the local population to the Catholic faith. Hindu temples were destroyed and brahmin priests fled to the secluded Ponda valleys, where today Goa's most important temples are found. By the end of the sixteenth century Goa reached its peak of military, social and ecclesiastical splendour. However, in the seventeenth century, threats from the neighbouring Marathas, epidemics and loss of trade compelled the Portuguese to desert Old Goa and move their capital to Panaji, at the mouth of the Mandovi River.

Meanwhile, new European rivals arrived in India — the Dutch, the French and finally, the British who ruled

India until its independence in 1947. Even when India achieved independence, the Portuguese government refused to part with Goa. The relationship between the two countries deteriorated until in December 1961, the Indian Prime Minister, Jawaharlal Nehru, ordered Indian forces to invade Goa. The Portuguese surrendered and after four and a half centuries of Portuguese rule, Goa became a part of India. Independence proved beneficial to Goa and brought substantial planned investment, modernisation and development.

Goa's climate is ideal. From late September until end March days are warm and sunny. Nights are cooler with little or no rain. April and May are definitely hot and during the heavy monsoon months of July and August, very few people visit Goa.

Just over 30 percent of Goa's people are Christians, most of them Roman Catholics and the state is dotted with beautiful churches. Goa's Hindu population predominate in the inland rural communities, where one can see the characteristically colourful temples.

The impact of 450 years of Portuguese rule is evident in Goa and makes it culturally very different from the rest of India. Goan cuisine is a mixture of Portuguese and Indian traditions, and wine, drunk very little elsewhere in India, is available everywhere. Goans are India's first exponents of pop music and even traditional folk dances in Goa have been influenced by European customs.

Goans are addicted to sport, especially football, again because of the Portuguese influence, and many Goans are selected for India's national soccer team

What makes Goa completely unique from the rest of India is its idyllic charm and laid-back atmosphere – its ambience, a successful blend of European and Indian cultures. The Goans are friendly, hospitable people and their attitude is truly in tune with the natural beauty that surrounds them.

Goa's palm-fringed coastline

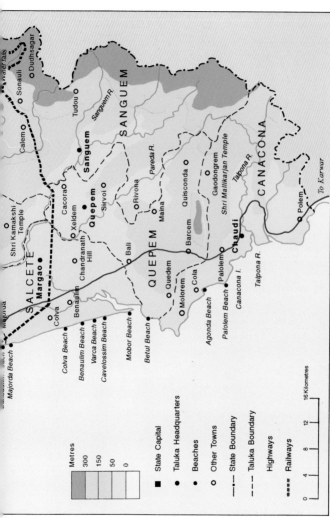

Coastline and borders shown on this map are neither authentic nor correct.

Metres
300
150
50
0

■ State Capital
● Taluka Headquarters
● Beaches
○ Other Towns
–·–·– State Boundary
– – – Taluka Boundary
▬▬▬ Highways
▬▬▬ Railways

0 4 8 12 16 Kilometres

Top: *Chapora Fort*; Below: *Cabo de Rama Fort*.

Top: *Deshprabhu House;* Below: *Mangesh Temple*

Fishing trawlers along the coast

A

ACCOMMODATION

Goa offers a large range of accommodation to cater to various pockets. It ranges from luxurious five-star hotels to basic dormitories. There are many hotels, apartments, guesthouses, cottages, dormitories and suchlike, depending upon the budget and expectations of the tourists.

The hotels offer very good service and good value for money. Most of them offer the guests free airport transfers and a free coach ride into town on weekdays. Many offer tours by coach to various places of archaeological and scenic importance, or take the guests on boat cruises. Most have their own swimming pools. Other sports facilities are also available at a nominal cost.

A range of accommodation is listed below:

North Goa

Aguada Holiday Resort Apartments and Guesthouse, Candolim (tel: 276071), is an apartment styled resort, five minutes' walk from the Aguada stretch of beach. The apartments are simply furnished but quite spacious. Each has a bedroom, living room, bathroom, kitchen with a fridge and a few utensils.

Aldeia Santa Rita, Candolim (tel: 277447), is just 250 metres from the beach, and has a homely village feel to it. Accommodation is in small villa-type buildings leading to the swimming pool.

Alfran Hotels, Calangute (tel: 276266), is a friendly hotel built in Portuguese style and is a 15-minute stroll from the beach. Accommodation here is arranged in the form of pretty building blocks around the pool, bar and terrace restaurant.

Alphaville Holiday Resort, Calangute (tel: 276011), on the edge of Calangute village, is just a five-minute brisk walk from the beach.

Altrude Guesthouse, Candolim, is newly built in a

cluster of guesthouses and restaurants and is five minutes' walk from the sea; spacious rooms, some with balconies, all with ceiling fans.

Annette Resort, between Baga and Calangute, is set on the east side of the Baga-Calangute road lined with shops, cafés and restaurants, the beach is a five-minute walk; all 70 rooms with balcony or terrace and ceiling fans; swimming pool, barbecues, live music; exceptional staff.

Beira Mar Alran Resorts, Baga (tel: 276246), is situated close to the beach, at the edge of Baga village. The hotel has 60 simply furnished rooms built around a central lawn area. The hotel has a swimming pool and the Meat & Loaf Restaurant which is good.

Casa Domani, Calangute, is very peaceful with a strong Goan flavour, found down a path seven minutes' walk from Calangute village centre; nine clean, functional rooms with ceiling fans, small swimming pool, breakfast served in the gardens.

Cavala, Baga (tel: 276090), is a peaceful Portuguese building full of character; looks towards the beach (two minutes' walk) one way and across fields the other; all 25 rooms with balcony and ceiling fans; good food in the garden restaurant.

Colonia Santa Maria Leisure Resort, Calangute (tel: 276491), or the CSM as it is known, looks more like a hamlet than a hotel. Though very close to Calangute Beach, it also has a swimming pool. Each room has a living area which allows for an extra bed.

Coqueiral Holiday Home Guesthouse, Calangute (tel: 250242), is a pleasant guesthouse near Candolim Beach, set in well kept gardens shaded by palm trees. Spotlessly clean; breakfast is served in the garden. Its manager, Mrs Braganza, also oversees neighbouring Schuberts and Palm Springs.

Dona Alcina Resorts, Candolim (tel: 276266), is peaceful yet three minutes' walk from the beach, run by devoted owner; all 124 rooms with balcony or terrace and ceiling fans; swimming pool, two excellent restaurants.

Falcon Resorts, Calangute, is a well–established hotel known for its personalised and friendly service. It has 24 a/c condominiums, 14 double bed family suites and 14 a/c antique rooms. The bedrooms are spacious with king-sized canopied beds, antique furniture and traditional furnishings. In the grounds there is a guitar-shaped swimming, wading and kids' pool.

Holiday Beach Resort, Candolim (tel: 276088), is an immaculate guesthouse, less than five minutes' walk from the beach.

Hotel Goan Heritage, Bardez (tel: 276253-54/ 276027), about 2.5 kilometres from Calangute Beach, has a restaurant and a shack on the lawns and a 'leisure centre', which includes reflexology, aerobics, yoga, etc.

Hotel Linda Goa, Baga (tel: 276066), is a charming old-fashioned hotel about a ten-minute walk from Baga Beach, with an open-air garden restaurant and rustic ambience.

Lua Nova Guesthouse, Calangute (tel: 276288), halfway between Hotel Ronil and the river, it is a five- minute walk over the sand dunes to Baga Beach. Patrick, the Goan manager, looks after his guests well. The back of the hotel overlooks paddy fields.

Mira Guesthouse, Calangute (tel: 277342), a comfortable, family run guesthouse, about six minutes' stroll from Calangute Beach.

Nilaya Hermitage, Arpora (tel: 276792), created by Claudia Derain, is new and ultra-swish. The few rooms may lack air-conditioning but the international jetset guests are more than adequately compensated by the superb architecture, pool and excellent food.

Palm Springs Guesthouse, Calangute, is a simple yet comfortable guesthouse. The beach is just across the lane that separates the Palm Springs from the Coqueiral, where breakfast is served.

Resorte de Santo Antonio, Calangute, is close to the chapel of St Anthony. It has 30 rooms and a cosy, poolside restaurant.

Sainto Antonio Hotel, Candolim, is across the road from the local church, with very warm atmosphere, five minutes' walk from the beach; all 40 rooms with balcony, fridge and ceiling fans; swimming pool and live music.

Schuberts Manor Guesthouse, Candolim, is across the lane from Coqueiral and is built as an old colonial villa, with roof terrace; most rooms with balcony or terrace, all with ceiling fans; breakfast at the Coqueiral or, on request, in bed; beach is three minutes' walk down lane.

Surfside Guesthouse, Candolim (tel: 276900). Close to the Coqueiral, and facing Candolim Beach, with its own cosy little restaurant.

Tamarind Lodge Hotel on Mapusa Road has no phone. It is a lovely rustic stone built hotel, in a very quiet spot some three kilometres from Anjuna and about 30 minutes' walk from the beach, but there is a courtesy beach bus.

The Riverside Guesthouse, Baga (tel: 276062). Somewhat spartan yet comfortable, situated on the banks of the Baga River about four minutes' walk from the beach. The setting is very ethnic, with paddy fields on one side. The hotel's restaurant is known for its inventive menu, which keeps changing, depending on what fresh produce is available in the local market that day.

The Taj Group of Hotels, Sinquerim, Bardez. There are three five-star hotels in all: The Fort Aguada Beach Resort, The Taj Holiday Village and The Aguada Hermitage. Guests staying in one can use the facilities of the others including half a dozen excellent restaurants plus cafés and bars.

The Aguada Hermitage (tel: 276201, fax: 276044), has 15 luxurious, stand alone villas, all of which have an uninterrupted view of the Arabian Sea from their location atop the Aguada hillock. These two or three bedroom villas are luxuriously furnished.

The Fort Aguada Beach Resort (tel: 276202), is built on the lines of a Mediterranean beach resort. It has terraced suites, standard rooms and cottages set among palm–shaded lawns.

The Taj Holiday Village (tel: 276201), has 144 villas. The villas are all set in a large coconut plantation opening directly onto Sinquerim Beach, designed to be like a rustic Goan village. The villas are whitewashed with *balcaõs* and red roof tiles. The villas are one, two, four and eight roomed.

Vagator Beach Resort, Anjuna (tel: 273277), covers about 50 acres of land, some of which is hilly, with steps leading down to the beach. The rooms facing inland look up to Chapora Fort. Rooms nearer the beach are a simple bungalow type. A five-minute walk up some steep steps leads to the hotel's swimming pool and more rooms. There are two restaurants, one beachside and the other poolside.

Villa Goesa Beach Resort Guesthouse and Hotel, Calangute (tel: 276182), lies between Baga and Calangute beaches and is about three minutes' from the sand. It comprises two whitewashed buildings surrounded by well kept gardens and two good restaurants.

Whispering Palms Beach Resort, Calangute (tel: 276141), is set in lovely gardens leading to Candolim Beach. This hotel is casual and yet quite elegant with rooms in the main building or in ten cottages around the swimming pool, each with private balconies. The hotel's restaurant is Lanai. Besides the swimming pool there is also a health club and an array of watersports facilities.

Xavier's Beach Resort Guesthouse, Baga (tel: 276048). Just a few kilometres from the beach this guesthouse is more like a little hotel. A gourmet's paradise, as Xavier (the owner) is also the excellent chef of his restaurant.

Other hotels:
A' Canoa, Calangute Beach, tel: 276082
Bambolim Beach Resort, Nunes Beach, Bambolim, tel: 246647
Calangute Beach Resort, Unta Vaddo, tel: 276063
Grandpa's Inn and Hotels, Anjuna, tel: 273271

Hotel Baia Do Sol, Baga, tel: 276084
Hotel Bareton, near Head Post Office, Luis Menezes Road,
Hotel Blue Bay, Caranzalem Beach, Miramar, Panaji,
tel: 46981
Hotel Delmon Caetano, Albuquerque Road, Panaji,
tel: 225616
Hotel Fidalgo, 18th June Road, Panaji, tel: 226291
Hotel Golden Goa, Dr Atmaram Borkar Road, Panaji,
tel: 223204
Hotel Hacienda, Saunta Vaddo, Baga, tel: 277348
Hotel Mandovi, P B 164, D B Marg, Panaji, tel: 226270
Hotel Nova Goa, Dr Atmaram Borkar Road, Panaji, tel: 46231
Hotel Orfil, Porba Vaddo, Calangute, tel: 27611
Hotel Palacio De Goa, Gama Pinto Road, Panaji, tel: 44289
Hotel Ronil Royale, Baga-Calangute Road, tel: 276183
Hotel Santiago, Baga, tel: 276564
Hotel Shelsta, Cobra Vaddo, tel: 27-6069
Hotel Solmar, D B Marg, Miramar, Panaji, tel: 226555
Hotel Villa Bomfim, Baga, tel: 276105
Keni's Hotel, 18th June Road, Panaji, tel: 224581
Osborne Resorts Private Limited, Gaura Vaddo, Calangute,
tel: 263260
Palma Rinha, Calangute, tel: 250190
Panjim Inn, E-212 Fontainhas, tel: 226523
Summer Ville, Dando, Candolim, tel: 262681

South Goa
Cidade de Goa Beach Resort, Vainguinim, Dona Paula
(tel: 221133), is family-run and very friendly. Its Goan
architect, Charles Correa, designed it like a Portuguese
fishing village. The rooms open on the terraces and
courtyards, and extensive gardens wrap right around the
whole of the small beach. No hawkers or beach shacks;
large pool, children's pool, large bar, six restaurants and
plenty of water sports available. The casino and
Beachoteque disco are added attractions.

   El Mar Beach Resort, Bogmalo (tel: 221274), is in

humble settings with plain, newly renovated rooms, attached baths and a small covered verandah with a restaurant.

Gaffino's Guesthouse, Mobor, Cavelossim (tel: 246385), is the smallest of Mobor's hotels with 16 rooms, all of which have good river views. Family-run, it is a five-minute walk from the beach. The restaurant is very popular with people staying in the more expensive hotels nearby.

Goa Renaissance Resort Hotel, Varca (tel: 745208/245218-08). Quality architecture and Mario Miranda's Goa village lobby relief surround the huge pool with built-in bar, leading to large garden with plenty of shade and then a path to an endless beach; all 118 rooms (including suites and villas) have air-conditioning, balcony, double beds, all bathrooms with bathtub; large swimming pool, five restaurants, three bars, casino and extensive sports facilities.

Goodfaith Lodge, Majorda village (tel: 254322), is ten minutes' from the beach and offers simple en-suite rooms with fans and small balconies.

Holiday Inn Resort, Mobor, Cavelossim (tel: 246303), is a three-star place with 144 double rooms arranged around a pool. All rooms have attached baths. There are two conference halls, two restaurants, a 24-hour coffee shop, health club, tennis court.

Joets Guesthouse, Bogmalo, is a well-established, hospitable place right on the beach with a sea-front restaurant. It has been recently refurbished. All rooms have ceiling fans and large attached bathrooms.

Leela Beach Resort, Mobor, Cavelossim (tel: 246363), has spacious villas set amid 45 acres of lawns and has seven multi-cuisine restaurants, a disco, a huge pool and superb sports and leisure facilities. The main building is airy and catches the sea-breeze.

Majorda Beach Resort, Majorda (tel: 220025), has lush, well kept gardens with all 120 rooms opening onto a balcony. Rooms have air-conditioning and a fridge. There are some individual cottages on the grounds. There are two swimming pools, one indoors, two restaurants, barbecues, extensive sports facilities and a regular live dance band which add to the charm.

Regency Travelodge Hotel, Majorda, is a member of the Southern Pacific Hotel Group. Friendly atmosphere, the extensive grounds lead to a mango grove with a path to the almost empty beach; all 200 rooms air-conditioned, satellite TV; large swimming pool and excellent restaurant.

Resorte de Goa, Varca (tel: 245066), has 56 double rooms including five suites with attached baths. The other facilities include a swimming pool, a tennis court, pool bar and beach bars.

Vinny's Holiday Guesthouse, Bogmalo (tel: 510174). Splendid hospitality up on the hillside, a 15-minute walk from the beach (a complimentary bus avoids the walk back up). All rooms with terrace and ceiling fans.

William's Beach Resort and Guesthouse Colva (tel: 221077/733964). A five-minute stroll from Colva Beach, the Willaim's or Old Bill as its guests love to call it, is peacefully situated near Colva village. Some rooms have air-conditioning.

Other hotels:
Dona Sylvia, Mobor, Cavelossim, tel: 246321
Hotel Park Plaza, Bogmalo, tel: 513291
La Ben, Colva Beach, tel: 732009
Molyma Hotels, Kindlebaga, Canacona, tel: 643028
Old Anchor Apartment Hotel, Mobor, tel: 223005
Prainha Cottages by the Sea, Dona Paula, tel: 224162
Santos Resorts, Bati Curtorim, Salcete, tel: 735400
Sea Queen Resorts Private Limited, Colva, tel: 720499
Silver Sands, Colva, tel: 221645
Swimsea Beach Resort, Dona Paula-Caranzalem Beach, tel: 225422
Villa Sol Hill Resort, Dona Paula, tel: 225045

AIRLINES

National : Since the Indian government's 'open skies policy' came into effect, Indian Airlines no longer dominates the Indian skies. Today, a wide choice of air taxis compete with each other to provide excellent service, and more importantly, punctuality and reliability.

Air taxis operating to and from Goa, with offices in Panaji include:

Jet Airways, 102 Rizvi Chambers, Ist Floor, Caetano Albuquerque Road, tel: 224471–6

Indian Airlines, Dempo House, Dayananad Bandodkar Marg, tel: 223826, (airport) 513863

Sahara, Hotel Fidalgo, 18th June Road, tel: 226291

Skyline NEPC Limited, Liv In Apartments, Behind Hotel Delmon, tel: 229233, 220192, 223730

International: Air India flies weekly direct into Goa from the Gulf. Besides these, there are also the international charter planes (Inspirations, Hayes & Jarvis, Larsen Reiser, Somak, Distant Dreams, etc) arriving from Europe and the USA.

The various international airlines which have their offices at Panaji, are:

Air France, tel: 226154

Air India, Hotel Fidalgo, 18th June Road, tel: 224081

Quantas, tel: 226154

Biman Bangladesh, tel: 226154

British Airways, 2 Excelsior Chambers, M G Road, tel: 224573

Gulf Air, tel: 226154

Kuwait Airways, tel: 43891

Philippine Airways, tel: 226154

AIRPORT

Dabolim Airport is close to Mormugao Port and the industrial town of Vasco da Gama. It is a combined naval and civil air station, approximately 29 kilometres from the capital city, Panaji. Transport to and from the airport to any destination in Goa is by taxi or bus. Telephone: (0834) 512644.

ANIMALS

The Slender Loris is occasionally found in the dense forests of Molem and Canacona. In the monkey family, the Bonnet Macaque and the Common Langur are frequently spotted.

Tigers are rarely found, but stray ones occasionally wander in from the neighbouring forest. Other cats — Leopard, Jungle Cat, Leopard Cat and the Common Palm Civet — are sometimes sighted. The Mongoose is found near habitations, while the Sloth Bear has on rare occasions attacked human beings in Surla Ghat and in Cotigao. Jackals are usually seen at night, sometimes roaming the hills by day as do Stripped Hyenas and Wild Dogs.

At dusk the Fulvous Fruit Bat, the Rufous Horseshoe Bat, the Dormer's Bat and the Malay False Vampire fly about. Flying Foxes and Short–nosed Fruit Bats are more rare.

The Indian Giant Squirrel attracts the attention of visitors to the forest by its peculiar call. It is commonly found in the forests of Molem, Valpoi and Canacona. The Three-stripped Palm Squirrel, the Five-stripped Palm Squirrel and the large brown Giant Flying Squirrel are also found in Goa.

In the rodent family one can find the Indian Field Mouse, the common House Rat, the Indian Gerbil, bandicoots, Blanford's Rat and the House Shrew.

The Indian Porcupine is renowned for damaging teak and cashew seedlings. Hare are found on grassy banks. The Indian Bison, which is the state animal of Goa, is usually found in herds in the Cordal Valley, Molem and Canacona.

Among the antelopes there are Sambar, Chital, Barking Deer, Mouse Deer and Hay Deer.

Wild Boars are particularly fond of cashew fruits. They also damage paddy, banana and sugarcane crops and are dreaded by farmers in the ghat areas.

Sea mammals include the Sea Cow, tortoise and the Long-beaked Dolphin. The Common Otter and the Smooth Indian Otter are found in the rivers and lakes.

ART GALLERIES

Kala Academy, Panaji (tel: 228254). Goa's centre for art and culture, plays, dramas, *tiatro* (Goan plays) and art exhibitions was established in 1969 at Campal, which leads to the Miramar Beach. The Academy complex is also worth visiting for its architecture, which has been designed by Goa's best known architect, Charles Correa.

Kerkar Art Gallery, Calangute (tel: 276017). This gallery belongs to the Kerkar family, who are well known artists of Goa. It houses water-colours, and oil paintings by prominent Indian artists. The complex also houses a studio for sculpture and a shop selling handicrafts. Concerts of Indian classical music and dance are normally held on Tuesdays and Saturdays at 6.30 pm.
Open: Monday to Saturday; 10 am to 7 pm.

Renaissance, Panaji (tel: 223023). This gallery is in Rebello Mansion across the road from the Kala Academy at Campal. It holds regular exhibitions of paintings, sculpture and pottery and has an emporium for handicrafts and a small café.

The Flying Dutchman Art Gallery, Calangute (tel: 277437). This gallery, which is on the Calangute-Baga Road, displays the works of various international as well as local artists. On Saturday evenings all art lovers gather here over snacks and drinks.
Open: Daily; 10 am to 1 pm and 4 to 10 pm.

Xavier's Centre of Historical Research, Panaji (tel: 217722). This centre houses a library and an art gallery. It is situated on Torda Road.

ARTISANS

The goldsmiths, or *shetties* as they are called in Goa, work in both silver and gold. Among the jewellery unique to Goa are the famous 'marquesite' sets used by Christian women for weddings and green malachite chains, earrings and rings which are in fashion even to this day. The jewellery worn by Hindu women is much more intricate and ornate. They make less use of precious stone; instead, black beads are used.

The *kumars* (potters) mainly work on objects that have a practical use in everyday life. Of late the artisans have been using their knowledge and expertise to make moulded sculptures, decorative vases and cladding tiles. One of India's famous potters, Zilu Harmalkar, has his studio at the Bicholim Industrial Estate.

Other ethnic Goan items include lacquered wooden articles produced by the *chittaries* from Cansaulim in South Goa, brassware and copperware articles made by the *kansars* (coppersmiths), and eco-friendly products like coconut shell carvings, banana fibre bags, jute products and bamboo mats and baskets.

B

BANKS (see CREDIT CARDS, page 61)

Goa is well serviced by banks. Most major nationalised banks have branches in Panaji and in some of the larger villages. And most banks, especially in Panaji, offer foreign exchange and encash travellers' cheques. There is only one foreign bank in Goa, the Standard Chartered Bank in Vasco. Banking hours are normally short, 10 am to 1 pm (noon on Saturdays).

Some of the **nationalised banks** in Goa include:
Corporation Bank
Dena Bank
Karnataka Bank
Punjab National Bank

State Bank of India
United Western Bank

Private cooperative banks include:
Centurion Bank
Goa Urban Cooperative Bank
Mapusa Urban Cooperative Bank
Saraswat Cooperative Bank
Vyasya Bank

BARGAIN

India has an array of exotica to satisfy the most
discriminating souvenir hunter. Items combine good
design, marvellous colour and elegant usefulness, others
may look perfect in a romantic Indian setting, but not
quite so well on your mantlepiece or hall table at home.
We have no warning to proffer; we just suggest that before
you take a tumble for some irresistable object, picture it in
its eventual setting, then you will come away with the
best India has to offer.

To haggle or not to haggle, this entirely depends upon
you. There are state-run emporia which sell good quality crafts
at fixed prices but these are found only in cities. For local
colour, you have to haggle if you want a bargain.

The street-peddler will usually ask about three times
the price he hopes to get, so always ensure that the first
price you offer is 25 percent of his first quote, working
up to 50 percent as a maximum. It is best to decide
beforehand how much the object is worth to you and of
course to remember that the seller has been doing it
longer than you!

If you are tempted to haggle and walk away with a
'bargain', please do not ask your neighbours how much
they paid for the same article as it may shatter your illusions!

BARS (see DRINKS and FENI, pages 66 and 72)

Goans have acquired a love for wine from their Portuguese
rulers. Hence, unusual in India, Goa abounds in bars.

Most restaurants have a permit to serve alcohol. Street
corners, markets and beach shacks have drinking areas
earmarked for those who want to pep up their spirits.

BATTERIES
All standard sized batteries are available in Goa at general
stores. Special batteries for cameras, etc, are sold at most
of the photographic studios, such as Souza Paul
Photographers on M R Road, opposite the Government
Printing Press, Panaji.

BEACHES
Goa's prime attraction to holidaymakers, both Indian and
foreign, is its 106-kilometre-long palm–fringed coastline.
Goa's coastline has lovely stretches of beaches studded
with luxury resorts, charming beach shacks and secluded
coves. Beaches range from good to superlative. All have
fine stretches of silver sand, unbroken for several
kilometres. The longest stretch of unbroken beach is about
20 kilometres in South Goa, from Velsao to Mobor called
the *uba dando*.

The beaches in North Goa are more popular and well
known. But the southern beaches are less crowded, cleaner
and whiter.

North Goa
Arambol — Chapora — Vagator — Anjuna — Baga —
Calangute — Candolim — Sinquerim. This stretch
comprises some of the most popular beaches in Goa. They
have beautiful scenery and are quite accessible to the
tourist. This is also the most crowded part of Goa, with
plenty of accommodation ranging from guesthouses to
luxury hotels. Along the shore, beach shacks serve fresh
seafood and equipment can be hired for water sports such
as angling, para-sailing, sailing, water-skiing, wind surfing
and diving.

MAHARASHTRA

R. Terekhol

Querim Beach

Pernem
Malpem
Alorna

Arambol
(Harmal) Beach

Mandrem Beach

Colvale

Morgim Beach

Assonora

Chapora
Vagator Beach
Anjuna Beach

Mapusa

Bicholim

Baga Beach

Calangute

Calangute Beach

R. Mapusa

Candolim Beach

R. Mandovi

Singuerim Beach

Aguada Fort

Miramar(Gasper Dias) Beach

Caranzalem Beach

Dona Paula Beach

Vainguinim Beach

PANAJI
Old Goa
Corlim

Siridao Beach

MORMUGAO BAY

Vasco da Gama

Cortalim

Dabolim

R. Zuari

Bogmalo Beach

Velsao Beach
Cansaulim Beach

Verna

Majorda Beach

● Beaches

○ Other towns

— Roads

--- Railway

Beaches of
NORTH GOA

0   5   10

Kilometres

Coastline and borders shown on this map are neither authentic nor correct.

Arambol (Harmal) Beach, about 50 kilometres northwards from Panaji, the capital city, is a quiet beach with a fresh water lake right on the shore.

Vagator Beach, dominated by Chapora Fort on the northern side, is still a hippies' haven. It comprises of two sandy bays north of Anjuna. **Anjuna**, the hangout of the hippies and the flower children of the 1960s, retains its informal atmosphere and has a weekly flea market every Wednesday.

Baga, the next beach on this stretch, is very popular. Here a fresh water rivulet of the same name meets the sea. A popular tourist resort, comfortable accommodation and good-quality restaurants are available at a short distance from the beach which has clean white sand.

Calangute, one of the most popular beaches in Goa, is about 16 kilometres from Panaji. In the woods and coconut groves behind the beach, hide small houses with family holiday accommodation. It is Goa's most crowded beach, filled with all kinds of eating joints from beach shacks to restaurants. Picturesque fishing boats dot the seascape. Package tourists now predominate.

Candolim is the next beach. This beachfront is almost as broad as it is long. Some good refreshment shacks are found here.

Sinquerim, the first beach north of the Mandovi River, is also the site of Aguada Fort, one of the best preserved Portuguese coastal forts. Fort Aguada Beach Resort, one of the cluster of three Taj Group hotels, is also here. Just beyond the fort is the lighthouse built in 1864. A new lighthouse outside the complex replaced the function of the original.

Miramar, Dona Paula and Bambolim: These are three beaches which lie between the North and South beaches.

Miramar Beach, or Gaspar Dias Beach as it was originally called, is the closest one to the capital. It is three kilometres west of Panaji towards Dona Paula. It is not safe for swimming as it is badly polluted but is still quite popular among the Indian tourists. Every year, in November, the Goa Tourism Department hosts a Food and Music Festival on this beach. The locals play their favourite sport, football, on the wide stretch of sand.

Dona Paula Beach, just seven kilometres from Panaji, is well wooded and offers a wide variety of water sports. The beach runs around in a bay to **Vainguinim Beach** where the Cidade de Goa, one of Goa's largest hotels, stretches along much of it. The beach is totally safe from beach traders. The Jesuits had occupied this area towards the end of the 16th century. It was an orchard, watered by two springs, that were surrounded by an areca grove. The bay abounded with exotic flora which the Jesuits had introduced from their travels abroad. There were fruit bearing trees of all kinds. Later, with the help of an efficient lift irrigation system and a canal, the cultivation of rice in the dry season was undertaken, which is called *vaingon* (kharif crop). The bay was also the home for different animals, both domesticated and wild. There was abundant seafood, especially crabs or *culleo* as they are locally called. The combination of these two (ie the *culleo* and the *vaingon*) resulted in the local people giving the bay the name 'Culleovaingon' or 'Curla-vangni'.

Bambolim Beach is five kilometres from Panaji, towards South Goa, via the village of Santa Cruz. It is very popular among early morning swimmers, and is also considered a lovely spot for a picnic.

South Goa

In Mormugao taluka there are a string of excellent beaches like the Bogmalo, Hollant, Cola, Pale, Velsao and Cansaulim. But it is further south in the Salcete taluka that Goa's widest and cleanest beaches like Majorda, Betalbatim, Benaulim, Colva, Cavelossim, Mobor, Betul and Palolem are situated.

Majorda Beach is part of the stretch of villages along the uninterrupted beach from Velsao to Mobor. Here you will find stately homes built by the descendants of the rulers of ancient times. As you walk along this secluded beach you will find a variety of sea life such as bivalves, sea-urchins and starfish. Luxury accommodation is available a short stroll from the village to the sea.

Colva Beach is approximately eight kilometres from Margao, the commercial centre of South Goa. It is the most popular beach of South Goa and hence the most crowded and, like Calangute in the North, has a number of good beach shacks. On weekends and festivals the beach gets fairly crowded.

Benaulim Beach is another secluded beach, along the southern coast of Goa. Here the fishermen of the village may be seen wearing their traditional red loin cloth, held up by a silver waistband. Water sports facilities are available on this beautiful white sand beach though developers are moving in quickly, but comparatively empty stretches lie between a two-mile walk on either side.

Cavelossim and **Mobor** are near a number of de-luxe hotels. Both beaches are famous for their cleanliness and their white sand. The sea also provides a rich variety of fish, and it is at nearby **Betul** that Goa's largest mussels are brought ashore by divers. By walking southwards along Mobor Beach, tourists will pass villagers laying out thousands of tiny fish for drying on the sand. The inlet of River Sal lies here.

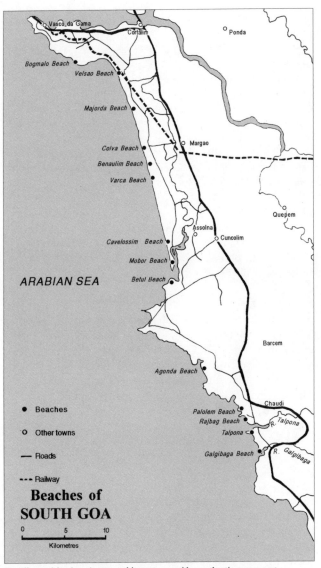

Beaches of SOUTH GOA

ARABIAN SEA

- ● Beaches
- ○ Other towns
- — Roads
- --- Railway

0   5   10
Kilometres

Coastline and borders shown on this map are neither authentic nor correct.

Palolem Beach is about 37 kilometres south of Margao. This C-shaped beach, with a backdrop of the Western Ghats, is one of Goa's most beautiful southern beaches. The hill at the north end is partly submerged at high tide to give the impression of an island in the middle of a calm lagoon. In the small village, accommodation is available in the form of tents and simple cottages. This beach has become one of the favourite sites for overnight beach picnics among the youth of Goa. At one end lies Canacona island, linked to the land by a causeway. Palolem village lies a hundred metres from the soft golden sands of the beach, to which it is connected by a short street.

BEACH BOYS

One of the outcomes of a brisk tourist business has been the increasing number of children on the beaches selling something in order to make a quick buck. Despite the smiles, bargain hard.

BEACH SHACKS

Beach shacks are a long-established institution in Goa, which, despite government and local hoteliers' efforts, will hopefully not go away. Traditionally, they were built and run by the café owners of the fishing villages lying behind the beaches, roughly constructed out of palm fronds. Alternatively, shacks would be improvised out of fishermen's beach huts built for drying and mending nets and sorting the fish.

Yet, today, these simple shacks are ideal places to relax, listen to music, eat and, of course drink.

BEGGING

India has a large number of beggars, although there are fewer in Goa than elsewhere. Many Indians give money to them for religious reasons. But on the whole, begging is a racket and the central government and local authorities are trying to wipe it out. For the traveller it is hard to resist a plea, especially from a child. But please remember, it is charity that turns children into beggars dependant upon the benevolence of the more fortunate. Travellers are encouraged to contribute instead to a well-run, reliable Indian or foreign charity.

Foreign visitors to Indian cities are often approached by 'students' or supporters of political parties who offer little paper flags in exchange for a 'contribution'. These requests should be politely resisted.

At temples, brahmin priests might approach you to give a blessing that involves touching your forehead with sandalwood paste and vermilion. A few rupees' donation to the temple are expected in exchange.

BIRDLIFE
Goa has a wide variety of magnificent birds. This large and diverse population can survive because of its varied habitat that ranges from open forests to shrubs, tracks and dense forests which are ideal for breeding. The following is a list of birds sighted in Goa:

Little Egret, Median Egret, Cattle Egret, Indian Reef Heron and the Paddybird are seen at water ponds and estuaries.

The Pallas's Fishing Eagle and the Brahminy Kite are frequently seen along the riverside. Others include Black Eagle, White-eyed Buzzard Eagle, Blackwinged Kite, Pariah Kite, Shikra, Sparrow Hawk, Serpent Eagle, Marsh Harrier, Shaheen Falcon and Osprey.

The King Vulture and the Whitebacked Vulture are the scavengers found here.

In the forests of Pernem and Satari you can find peafowls. Around the bamboo thickets of Molem, Valpoi and Canacona, Junglefowls and Jungle Bush Quails are found as also the Grey Quail, Indian Bustard Quail, Red Spurfowl and the Grey Junglefowl.

Pigeons include the Blue Rock Pigeon, Red Turtle Dove, Spotted Dove, Little Brown Dove, Greyfronted Green Pigeon, Imperial Green Pigeon, Nilgiri Wood Pigeon, Rufous Turtle Dove and the Indian Ring Dove.

Roseringed Parakeets, Blossomheaded Parakeets, Bluewinged Parakeets and the Indian Lorrikeet are seen near food crops and orchards in large numbers.

Cuckoos include Pied Crested Cuckoo, Indian Cuckoo, Indian Hawk Cuckoo, Plaintive Cuckoo, and the Drongo Cuckoos.

Owls include the Barn Owl, Spotted Owlet, Barred Jungle Owlet, Greateared Nightjar, Indian Jungle Nightjar, Longtailed Nightjar, Whiterumped Swift, House Swift and Palm Swift.

The Pied Kingfisher, Small Blue Kingfisher, Whitebreasted Kingfisher, Blackcapped Kingfisher and the Storkbilled Kingfisher are seen along water ponds and river fronts.

The Bluetailed Bee–eater, Chestnutheaded Bee–eater, Small Green Bee–eater and the Bluebearded Bee–eater are found mostly over the areas covered with paddy fields.

The Common Grey Hornbill, Malabar Grey Hornbill, Malabar Pied Hornbill and the Great Pied Hornbill are found in the forests in Valpoi.

The Bluethroated Barbet, Large Green Barbet, Small Green Barbet and the Crimsonthroated Barbet are also seen in the forests.

Goldenbacked Woodpecker, Rufous Woodpecker, Black Woodpecker, Pygmy Woodpecker, Heartspotted and the Large Goldenbacked Woodpecker are seen in Goa.

The Wiretailed and Redrumped Swallow are found here too.

The Grey Shrike, Rufousbacked Shrike, Brown Shrike, Ashy Swallow Shrike, Blackheaded Cuckoo Shrike, Pied Flycatcher Shrike, Large Wood Shrike, Common Wood Shrike, Large Cuckoo Shrike and Blackheaded Cuckoo Shrike are found.

The Golden Oriole, the Blackheaded Oriole, the Black Drongo, Racket-tailed Drongo, Grey Drongo, White-bellied Drongo, Bronzed and the Haircrested Drongos are also seen.

Among the mynas found are the Common, Hill, Rosy Paster, Greyheaded and the Jungle Mynas.

House Crows, Jungle Crow and Tree Pies are found throughout the state.

Green, Redvented, Whitecheeked, Redwhiskered, Greyheaded, Blackheaded, Yellowbrowed, Rubythroated, Whitecapped, and Black Bulbuls are found here.

Among the Babblers, the Spotted, Slatyheaded Scimitar, Blackheaded, Rufousbellied and the Quaker Babbler are seen. The Brownbreasted Flycatcher, Redbreasted, Whitebrowed Blue, Whitebellied Blue, Bluethroated, Verditer, Paradise and Blacknaped Monarch Flycatchers are visible.

Thrushes and warblers include Blueheaded Rock Thrush, Blue Rock Thrush, Malabar Whistling Thrush, Whitethroated Laughing Thrush. Ashy Wren Warbler, Tytler's Leaf Warbler, Largebilled Leaf Warbler, Magpie Robin, Shama, Redstart and the Indian Robin.

Sparrows include the Indian House Sparrow and the Yellowthroated Sparrow. The Common Weaver Bird is also widely seen.

Whitebacked and Blackheaded Munias, Purple and White-eyed Sunbirds, Indian Baya and Blackheaded Bunting and the Yellowcheeked Tit are also seen. Migratory waterfowls are found at the wetlands in Carambolim, Siroda and Corlim.

BIRD SANCTUARIES

The **Salim Ali Bird Sanctuary**, the only bird sanctuary in the state, extends across two square kilometres on the western tip of Chorao Island, at the mouth of River Mandovi and is covered with mangroves. Besides local and migratory birds, occasional sightings of foxes, crocodiles, turtles and jackals are possible. The island of Chorao also harbours crabs and molluscs. Herons, cranes, seagulls, egrets, kingfishers, junglefowl and the Paradise Fly Catcher are some of the 154 species of birds that have been spotted here. The sanctuary can be visited throughout the year, with the permission of the Chief Wildlife Warden, Forest Department, Junta House, Panaji, Goa. It is reached by the ferry going from Ribander to Chorao and then on foot. Private touring via canoes is also possible.

Also see WILDLIFE SANCTUARIES, which also have a good birdlife (pages 125).

BOOKSHOPS
Good bookshops in Goa keep plenty of English books published in India and abroad, often at low prices.

Panaji
Book Fair, situated at Hotel Mandovi on Dayanand Bandodkar Marg, tel: 224406
Singbal's Book Stall in the Communidade Building at Church Square, tel: 25747
Technical Book Centre, 2nd floor, Manjunath Building, 18th June Road, tel: 224052
Varsha Book Stall on Ormuz Road, opposite Azad Maidan, tel: 45832

Mapusa
The Other India Bookstore, above Mapusa Clinic, tel: 263305

Margao
Apna Ghar, Matruchaya Building, Cine Vishant Road, Malbhat, tel: 732250
Maya Book Stores, Vit-Rose Mansion, I B Road, tel: 221259
Nagesh Daivagna, Comba, behind Loyola High School, tel: 225537
Sambari Stores, Sambari House, Station Road, tel: 732450

Vasco
National Book Depot, Municipal Market, tel: 512659

Ponda
Nalanda, 2, Mahalakshmi Complex, near the Bus Stand, Curti, tel: 312443

Top: *Fort Aguada*; Below: *Tiracol Fort*.

Fishing activity on the beach.

Top: *A wedding ceremony*; Above: *Midnight Mass.*

Top: *Se Cathedral;* Below: *Calangute's church.*

BUSES

Buses are cheap and reach every corner of Goa. They are operated by the state-run Kadamba Transport Corporation (KTC) and by private bus operators. Most towns have their local bus depot. The major bus depots are at Panaji, Margao, Mapusa, Ponda and Vasco. Services are frequent and destinations written in English.

There are also bus services to destinations outside Goa run by KTC, other state governments and approved private operators.

Caution should be taken to see that tickets are purchased only from authorised agents or transport operators. Fare can also be paid on the bus. However, buses are fairly slow as they make frequent stops.

C

CAR HIRE

One can hire cars with or without drivers, although a driver is recommended. Prices are cheaper for cars without air-conditioning.

Agencies that hire out cars include:
Hertz Wheels Rent a Car, 9 Hotel Gladstone Building, F L Gomes Road, Vasco 403602, tel: 512297
Hertz Wheels Rent a Car, Shiv Krupa Building, Opposite Don Bosco High School, St Inez, Panaji, tel: 44304/43758
Om Kar Rentals, 3, Gomes Building, Behind Old Telegraph Office, Margao, tel: 220055
Skylark Cottages, Colva Beach, Colva, tel: 223669
Budget Rent a Car, Porvorim, tel: 217063

CHEMIST

See PHARMACY, page 98.

CHURCHES

Goa has truly earned the name 'Rome of the East'. It abounds in churches and chapels, some dating back to the

16th century. The profusion and architectural excellence of churches include superb examples of late Renaissance, early Baroque, Manueline and Gothic. These churches have very intricate detailing and ornamentation. The most popular or the best known are the churches and cathedrals at Old Goa. But these are definitely not the only ones worth mentioning. Here are some worth visiting. They will certainly be open on Sundays; other days are variable. The ones at Old Goa are open daily.

Basilica of Bom Jesus (Good Jesus), Old Goa. This imposing Basilica was built by the Jesuits, and consecrated to the Holy Name of Jesus on 15 May 1605. The mortal remains of St Francis Xavier are housed inside. Until the church was built, they were kept at St Paul's, Old Goa.

The casket holding the body of the saint was a gift of the Duke of Tuscany. The body of the saint is dressed in rich vestments with an embroidered coat of arms. On the right-hand side is a golden baton with 194 emeralds and at the feet is a big gold medal of King Dom Pedro II.

The Basilica's three-storey western front overlooks a forecourt which it shares with the 'Casa Professa' (Professed House) of the Jesuits. The imposing façade of black granite is remarkable for its simplicity. The first thing the visitor sees as he enters the church is the life size statue of St Ignatius of Loyola, the founder of the Jesuits, which occupies the centre of the main altar.

Before the Professed House was built, this area was a vast square known as 'Terreiro dos Galos' because cockfights were held here. The Professed House of the Jesuits was constructed in 1585, stoutly opposed by the Municipal Chamber of the city, the Santa Casa de Misericordia and the Franciscans. It was rebuilt in 1663, after a fire. The somewhat forbidding façade is linked to the Basilica of Bom Jesus by a beautiful arcaded courtyard. Today this building is occupied by only a few Jesuit fathers who hold retreats there for youngsters. The most important feature of the exterior of this Basilica is the west façade, more elaborately decorated than that of any other Goan church.

Chapel of St Anthony, Old Goa. This chapel, on the hill near the church of Our Lady of the Rosary, is dedicated to the patron saint of Portugal. It was the royal chapel. The statue of St Anthony was given the rank of captain of the army, with a salary due to his rank. This statue was even taken in solemn procession to the State Treasury Office where the treasurer would respectfully deposit, in the hands of the statue, the salary due to him.

Small in proportions, the chapel has only a nave with flanking passages. The main altar has a vaulted panelled ceiling similar to that of the church of St Francis of Assisi. Clerestory windows flood the nave with sunlight.

Chapel of St Catherine, Old Goa. As a small free-standing structure, it was the first place of worship ever to be erected in Goa after the reconquest in 1510. It was built in thanks for the victory against the Muslims and is dedicated to St Catherine because her feast day is on 25 November, the date of the reconquest.

Although small in size, this chapel was made a cathedral on 3 November 1534 and remained so until the new cathedral was built. Its façade is Renaissance, a style later amplified for the present cathedral built nearby. A placard on the enlarged structure implied that the gateway to the Muslim city's wall was located here. It was further rebuilt just before the Portuguese were expelled from Goa.

Church of the Holy Spirit, Margao. First built in 1564, it was burnt down by Muslims (1571) and later rebuilt only to be demolished again (1645). The final structure was completed in 1675, with a façade of Ionic columns flanked by two towers which are seen over Margao and its surroundings. The church has ten altars and two small chapels. One is dedicated to Archangel Michael, and the other to St Roque and St Peter.

Church of Our Lady of the Immaculate Conception, Panaji. Set in the heart of Panaji, this church was built around AD 1541. Originally a chapel, it was elevated to a church in AD 1600 and then renovated in AD 1619.

The bell of the church is second in size only to that of the Se Cathedral at Old Goa. The bell's size is explained by the fact that it was not originally in this church but was brought from the ruined Augustinian monastery in Old Goa.

At the base of the church is Church Square. Red laterite steps jointed in white create a dazzling pattern leading to the entrance of the church. The staircase was built in 1870. In the sanctuary, the three altar pieces are great examples of Baroque craftsmanship. A chapel in the church dedicated to St Francis Xavier is on the south side.

Church of Our Lady of Miracles, Mapusa. This church was built in 1594 over a destroyed temple. It has an exquisite Baroque façade, three altars, the main one is dedicated to Our Lady of Miracles and is richly carved, as is the pulpit. The ceiling is intricately patterned with strips of wood. The image of Nossa Senhora de Milagres (Our Lady of Miracles) is held in great veneration, both by Hindus and Christians alike. The Hindus consider her a sister of Lairaee at Sirigao. The church was restored after a disastrous fire in 1838, it was again damaged when the Portuguese tried to blow up the adjacent bridge in 1961 while resisting India's attempt to liberate Goa.

Church of Our Lady of the Mount, Old Goa. On the summit of a hillock opposite the Se Cathedral stands the Church of Our Lady of the Mount (Feast day, 8 September). Neat stone steps lead up to the top. This is where the artillery of Yusuf Ali Adil Shah fired from and decimated Alfonso de Albuquerque's forces, Albuquerque reconquered Goa in 1510 and commissioned Our Lady of the Mount as part of his votive offering for victory.

Although this church can hardly be called one of the architectural jewels of Goa, from its steps one gets a splendid view of the surrounding great churches.

Church of Our Lady of the Rosary, Old Goa. Also known as the Church of St Mary of Rosary, this church was built in 1543 on the Holy Mount (Monte Santo) close to the convents of St Monica and St Augustine. Its importance is that it stands on the exact spot from where the conqueror of Goa, Alfonso de Albuquerque, witnessed the reconquest of Goa in 1510. The church bears the following inscription placed there in 1931: *Deste alto assistiu Alfonso de Albuquerque em 25-11-1510, a reconquista de Goa* (From this hillock Alfonso de Albuquerque on 25 November 1510 witnessed Portugal's reconquest of Goa). This was Old Goa's parish church from 1543. St Francis Xavier would preach here in the evenings, ringing his little bell to attract large crowds. The church is the oldest complete structure to survive in Old Goa.

The church's architectural style is Manueline, a blending of later Gothic and Renaissance. It is similar to the churches in Portugal such as the Church of Madelena of Olivenca noted for its façade composed of large square towers. The ceiling of the church is wooden. The church's austere, Romanesque external simplicity contrasts with the internal richness of the late Gothic decoration. Inside lies the tomb of Dona Catarina, wife of the Viceroy Garcia de Sa, whose marriage St Francis Xavier is said to have celebrated. As a whole, the church marks the beginning of Indo-Portuguese art. As the church is open only on special occasions, few visitors are able to view the simple but delightful interior with its beamed roof.

Church of the Rosary or **Mae De Deus Church**, Saligao. This church, in fine neo-Gothic style, was built in 1873 amidst picturesque surroundings. The shrine of the miraculous statue of the Mother of God was brought from the ruins of the Convent of Mae De Deus, Old Goa. Young boys are prepared at the minor seminary here for eventual enrollment at Rachol.

Church of Reis Magos, Verem (Bardez). Set on the right bank of the Mandovi River, the church was built in 1555. It is dedicated to the Three Magi Kings. Three viceroys who died while on service in Goa are buried here. Every 6 January, the feast of Reis Magos is celebrated here. This was once the home of all dignitaries of the Franciscan order and their mission. It is built next to the Reis Magos fort which is entirely a prison now.

Church of St Anne (Santana), Talaulim. Dedicated to St Ana, the grandmother of Jesus Christ, this is Goa's best surviving Baroque church. It was completed in 1695 on the right bank of Siridao River not far from Pilar Seminary and has picturesque surroundings. The unique feature of this church is that it has hollow walls through which people could walk in secrecy for the purpose of confession. Best visited on Sundays as it is sure to be open.

Church of St Cajetan, Old Goa. Standing close to the ruins of the Viceregal Palace, this beautiful church was built by Italian friars of the Theatine order in 1656-6. Though the church is small, it is clearly inspired by the Basilica of St Peter in Rome. The external architecture is Corinthian, the interior Mosaico-Corinthian. In the middle of the nave, directly under the cupola, is a well which is covered except for a small opening. The green grass on the cupola is attributed to the moisture emanating from the well. The church was recently renovated for use by the Pastoral Centre for its liturgical services. It is the only surviving domed church in Goa.

Church of St Francis of Assisi, Old Goa. The convent and church of St Francis of Assisi is next to the Cathedral.

The church was first built in 1510 and rebuilt from 1521 onwards on the site of a mosque. It has the most beautiful interior of all churches in Old Goa, wonderfully enriched with gold, especially at the east end. The painted ceiling remains, as do the 17th-century wall-paintings in the chancel. Portuguese tombstones carpet the nave floor. A Manueline doorway and octagonal towers flanking the façade are the two unusual features in the style of the otherwise exclusively Baroque church.

Church and Convent of St Augustine, Old Goa. A lonely tower retaining its original height of 46 metres (150 feet) overlooks the old city. It is a mere skeleton of the old square towers and the great church which are now a heap of ruins covered by vegetation. Yet it is impressive.

This convent was built in 1572 by a dozen Augustinian friars on their arrival in Goa. After a decade the convent was rebuilt, mainly through the efforts of Fr. Gaspar de Sao Vicente, and dedicated to Our Lady of Grace. It became Goa's richest convent, with a massive adjoining church, whose vaulted nave was one of Goa's feats of construction.

During construction, the high vault fell down twice. However, the Italian architect, would not give up. When built a third time, he and his only son stood under the vault and asked for a heavy cannon to be fired to test the stability of the structure. It did not fall down — until much later. Then the bell, Goa's second largest, was removed from the belfry and transferred to the Church of Our Lady of the Immaculate Conception, Panaji.

Towards the south of the convent, the Novitiate of the Augustinians was an integral part of the convent, while the majestic 'Collegio do Populo' was for training younger brethren. It was linked to the Novitiate by a bridge over the Rua dos Judeus (Street of the Jews). This group of imposing Augustinian buildings were abandoned when the order was suppressed.

Church and Convent of St John of God, Old Goa. Built in 1685, right next to St Augustine, the church is dedicated to Our Lady of Good Success. It gradually declined in importance until 1834 when the building was bought by the nuns of St Monica to be used as residence for their chaplains and confessors. It is comparatively simple in style and was completely restored by the Portuguese just before they were expelled from Goa.

The church and convent is now occupied by Franciscan nuns who run an Old Age Home.

Church and Convent of St Monica, Old Goa. Although largely decayed now, this was Goa's only convent for nuns. It was started on the holy hill in 1606 but was finished only in 1627, because a fire destroyed the building in 1620. It took 15 years to rebuild. This vast church and convent met all the needs of the 150 cloistered nuns from the retreat of Nossa Senhora de Serra. It had vast corridors, vaulted ceilings, a courtyard called 'Vale de Liro' and a three-storey palazzo-style building containing nuns' cells, penance rooms and a dungeon.

The 'penitents', either voluntarily or through persuasion, flagellated and stigmatised themselves with ropes, leather straps and iron nails. The 'recalcitrants' were cast in the dungeon, and here the Rodeira — the nun who held the keys to the outer door of the cloister — dealt with them and they were jailed for life.

As you entered the nunnery, there was a turntable with a hand-bell by it. Until the 19th century, illegitimate children were deposited here in the dead of night. When the bell was rung , the Rodeira would turn the table through an opening in the wall, pull in the unwanted child and have it baptised. The turntable has long since been dismantled, the wall whitewashed and all memories of this practice physically erased. The 17th century frescos on the dome have also been destroyed.

Today, much decayed, it is Asia's largest training

centre for Catholic nuns. At present this building is also the Mater Dei Institute, used by nuns of various orders for their theological studies.

Se Cathedral, Old Goa. The imposing Se Cathedral was completed in the year 1631. Work had begun in 1562 and it took over 62 years to complete. The massive structure, the largest in Goa, is dedicated to St Catherine of Alexandria on whose feast day in 1510, Alfonso de Albuquerque defeated the Muslim army and repossessed the city of Goa. The tower on the right fell down in 1776 and has not been rebuilt. The cathedral site was earlier occupied by a mosque.

Its inspiration may be the cathedral at Porto Alegre in Portugal, although it differs in the plan of the apse and the transepts.

The façade rises 115.66 feet to the crowning cross. The exterior is built in half-Tuscan, half-Doric style, the inside in Mosaico-Corinthian. The nave is 72 feet high. Near the entrance is the Baptismal font where St Francis Xavier is said to have baptised thousands of Goan converts. The main altar is engraved with images of the martyrdom of St Catherine. The Chapel of the Blessed Sacrament is beautifully decorated. The north tower was lost in 1776 after being struck by lightning. The south tower accommodates what is known as the 'golden bell', due to its resonant tone.

Adjoining the Cathedral, on its northwestern side, stands the Old Palace of the Archbishop.

In the neighbourhood of the Cathedral was the famous Palace of Inquisition, the Senate House and the 'Estancia Real de Tobaco' or Royal Depot of Tobacco. Here you will also find the ruins of the Royal Palace and its gateway just in front of the Church of Divine Providence, or the Church of St Cajetan, as it is popularly known. The doorway suggests Indo-Muslim influence, and reminds one of Muslim tombs and mosques.

St Alex Church, Calangute. This is one of Goa's oldest churches, built in 1597 on the site of a Hindu shrine called Ravalnath, whose remains can still be seen. It overlooks the main road to Mapusa.

Other churches:
Church of Our Lady, Majorda
Church of Our Lady of Hope, Candolim
Church of Our Lady of Mercy, Colva
Church of Our Lady of the Snow, Rachol
Church of St John the Baptist, Benaulim
Church of St Laurence, Agassaim
St Lawrence, Fort Aguada

CINEMAS

Cinemas in Goa mainly show Hindi movies, though the more popular English movies are shown at some.
There are cinema halls in all the major towns. Panaji has the Ashok, Samrat, National and El Dorado. Margao's include Metropole, Blue Pearl and Cine Vishant. At Ponda there is only one cinema hall, Cine Aisha; Mapusa has two, the El Captain and Alankar. Calangute has Cine Vanessa. Local newspapers carry the cinema listings and latest information on what is being shown at the different cinema theatres.

CLIMATE

The climatic conditions of Goa are temperate, except during the monsoon, which lasts from June to September. The weather is pleasant and sunny. There are no extremes in temperature. There are no clear demarcations from one season to the other except for the monsoon. The average temperature varies between 25° C to 36° C. The average annual rainfall is approximately 325 cms, the average daily hours of sunshine is nine to ten hours in summer and three to five hours during the monsoon.

CLOTHING

The recommended clothing here is light cottons. In the months from June to October, it is advisable to carry a light sweater or wrap, especially if you intend moving about in the villages of Goa. Rain–wear is also a must in this season. Hotels provide a fast, reliable laundry service. Clothing is very cheap to buy and tailor throughout India.

COMMUNICATIONS

Post: Postcards and letters take a somewhat elasticated week or so to reach foreign destinations; de-luxe hotels sometimes collect the mail and have it posted from Mumbai which is faster. Postcards bought in hotels cost much more than in the village; larger hotels have stamp supplies, saving post office queues.

Parcels: Should you be sending home a big buy, such as a carpet, the shop will package it up for you but remember to measure it, sign it on the back and photograph it; as it is unaccompanied luggage, you must sign a special form (provided by the shop) to avoid paying duty.

Telephone: Goa is part of the ISD (International Standard Dial) system so phoning is direct dial. But it can be expensive. Hotels mark up at least 100 percent, often much more; check the rate with the operator before making a call. To avoid it, use the manned telephone booths charging standard rates in most shopping areas. To telephone abroad, dial 00 (international), the country code (UK is 44, US 1), the area code (minus 0 for UK numbers) and the telephone number, eg 00 44 181 822566.

Faxsimile: Many hotels have faxes, with the same mark-up as their telephones, so please do check. Again, there are cheaper ones in the shopping areas.

CONSULATES
Presently there are two consulates in Goa:

Federal Republic of Germany
Honorary Consul in Goa, c/o Cosme Matias Menezes
Group, Rua de Ourem, Panaji 403001.
Tel: (0832) 223261/62/63/64
Fax: (0832) 43265

Consulate General of Portugal
7/B Lake View Colony, Miramar, Panaji 403001.
Fax: (0832) 432652

Consulates are empowered to process travel documents for
all European Community nations except U K, Ireland and
Denmark.

British citizens should refer to the **British Consulate** in
Mumbai. The address and telephone numbers are:
4 Maker Chamber, Second Floor, 222 Chanda Lal Bajaj
Road, Nariman Point, Bombay 400021, P. O. Box 11714.
Tel: (022) 2830517/2832330

COURIER SERVICES
Though expensive courier services can also be used to
send important documents and packages to any
destination in the world. They are reliable and much
quicker than the ordinary parcel post. Some companies are:

Blue Dart Express Ltd, F03, Surerkar Mansion, Opp. Govt.
Printing Press, Above Goenkar Restaurant, Panaji, tel: 47768.
DHL Worldvide Express, Nagesh Apt, Opp. Trionara
Apts, Rua Conde de Sarzedas, Panaji, tel: 226487, 222758.
Elbee Express Service, 6 Confraria Bldg, Jose Falcao
Road, Panaji, tel: 46631.

CREDIT CARDS (see BANKS, page 28)
Most credit cards are honoured at the larger hotels, shops
and travel agents. Encashment facilities into Indian
currency are available at the following banks and agents:

Andhra Bank, Dr Atmaram Borkar Road, Near EDC
House, Panaji, tel: 223513
Bank of Baroda branches at Panaji, Mapusa, Anjuna,
Calangute, Vasco da Gama, Margao, Majorda, Benaulim,
Varca and Cavelossim
Central Bank of India, Nizari Bhavan, First Floor, Near
Cine National, Panaji, tel: 45389
Pheroze Feamroze and Co, HTL Fidalgo, 18th June Road,
Panaji, tel: 226291
Thomas Cook India Ltd, Dayanand Bandodkar Marg,
Panaji, tel: 221312
Trade Wings Ltd, Mascarenhas Building, 18th June Road,
Panaji, tel: 226201
Wall Street Finance Ltd, M G Road, opposite Azad
Maidan, Panaji, tel: 224117

CUISINE (see FOOD, page 87)
Like the people of Goa, Goan food is a blend of Eastern
and Western cuisine. The daily meal of every Goan,
regardless of his religion, is rice and curry.

Rice varies from the locally unpolished, parboiled,
brown variety to the Basmati rice from northern India.
Curry is made by grinding coconut together with spices
and adding fish, prawns or other seafood to give a rich
flavour. This curry is commonly called *koddy*. The colour
varies from golden yellow to ochre, depending on the
spices used.

The love for fish is specially pronounced among the
Hindus, since they normally do not eat beef or pork. There
are days when they observe a strict vegetarian diet, on
these days even onions are not used in the food. This

gravy, prepared without onion and fish is called *shivrak*.

Pure Goan Hindu dishes such as *khat khatem*, *moongachyo gathi*, *bangdeanchi uddamethi*, and sweets like *mangane, tausoli, pais, kheer* remained untouched by Portuguese influence.

However, Goan Christian cuisine is a rich blend of Portuguese and Oriental cuisine. For instance, *feijoado* is made of butter beans and spicy Goan sausages with some ground masala to give it a spicy taste. *Balchao* comes from Burma and is prepared by adding a preservative of tiny shrimps locally called *galmo*, which is ground in palm *feni* with garlic, chillies, pepper, etc. This shrimp paste is used for *balchao de peixe*, made of seer fish, and *balchao do porco*, made of pork. *Vindaloo* and *sorpotel*, modified names of Portuguese dishes, have also been accepted by Goans. These are served with *sannas*, delicious rice cakes fermented with toddy. *Leitao assado* is a stuffed pigling baked with spices. *Galinha cafreal* is a chicken stuffed with spices and roasted with butter. *Xacuti*, fish *recheiado* and *xecxec* are other spicy Goan dishes. *Chouric pao* or sausage bread is a lip-smacking snack. *Von, paysa* and *shirvio* are few of the basic Goan sweets.

The Christmas season turns Goa into a Paradise City for sweet lovers. There are *neureos*, a pastry with a rich coconut and cashew stuffing, *dodoll*, a thick black custard, *bols*, a sweet wheat flour cake, and *pinagre* made from the flour of brown rice pounded with coconut jaggery and grated coconut. But the best loved is *bibinca*, a mouth - watering delicacy made of eggs, coconut milk and sugar, baked layer upon layer over a slow coal fire. Among the other sweets left to us as our Portuguese legacy are the *bolo podre* (coconut cake), *suspiros* (almond cookies), *bolo russo* (walnut and almond cake with a cream filling), *bolo de nozes* (a nut cake), *ovos da Pascoal* (Easter eggs) and *pateis da nata* (cream puffs).

CURRENCY

Indian currency is based on the decimal system, with 100 paise to the rupee. Coins are in denominations of 5, 10, 20, 25 and 50 paise. One, two and five rupee coins are also in use. Notes are in 1, 2, 5, 10, 20, 50, 100 and 500 rupee denominations. Indian rupees may not be brought in nor taken out of the country. Exchange rates fluctuate against other currencies but £1 is roughly 60 rupees and $1 is approximately 36 rupees.

D

DANCES (see FESTIVALS, page 81)

Despite Western influence amongst the young people, some traditional Goan dances have survived.

Bhandap

A traditional dance performed by tribal women in the second half of the Hindu month, *Bhadrapada*.

Correndinho

A Portuguese peasant dance, popular among the Goan youth.

Dhekni

Mixture of folk culture and Western music, this is danced by Christian girls in full Indian dress. The music is Western; the dancers carry *pontis* (small clay bowls with a burning wick floating in oil) or *aartis* (oil lamps).

Fugdi

At festivals such as the Dhalo or Ganesh Chaturthi, women dance either in a circle or in rows, with hand gestures and claps.

Ghohemodani

Performed in parts of Bicholim and Pernem, this dance is about a mounted cavalier setting off to war. The cavalier is

dressed as a Rajput chieftain with a Peshawari *pugree*
(headdress). Two or eight dancers with hobby horses
fastened below their waists are his fierce escorts in this
war dance.

Goph & Tonyamel

Both these folk dances are related to the Kala festival
associated with Lord Krishna. Men dance them during the
Shigmo festival (March) in the districts of Sanguem, Ponda,
Canacona and Pernem. At Mangesh Temple, females dance
the Goph. The Tonyamel is confined to men and is
danced with sticks in hand.

Musalam Khel

Christians of Chandor perform this pestle dance on the
second day of the Carnival in February. Wearing a Yadava
costume, some wave the *Shivalinga* (phallic symbol of Shiva)
while others hold burning torches. One man is dressed up
as a bear. At the end, a *devadasi* (temple dancer) dances
up with water and broom, sweeps the dance ground and
smears wet clay over it. She receives a customary fee.

Virabhadra

Performed annually in some parts of Ponda, Sanguem and
at Sanquelim. The style is south Indian. One actor
represents Virabhadra, who was created from the matted
locks of Shiva. He dances with two swords in his hand.
Two men dance at his side and a whole group supports
them with dancing and shouting.

DEPARTURE TAX

All passengers departing from Goa to a foreign country,
have to pay a departure tax of Rs300 at the airport.

DOCTORS

Acupuncture

Dr Bipin Salkar, Kelkar Polyclinic, Minguel Furtado Road,
Comba, Vasco, tel: 513511

Ayurvedic, Unani and Nature Care
Dr Assis Fernandes, Ground Floor, Opposite Lohia Maidan, Margao, tel: 222082

Cancer
Dr Vithal Kamat Kelkar Polyclinic, Minguel Furtado Road, Comba, Margao

Cardiologists
Dr Antonio Dos Rodrigues Sterling Apartments, Pajifond, Margao, tel: 720925
Dr Arvind V Naik, P O 230, Padre Miranda Road, Margao, tel: 732580
Dr Dilip V Bhandare, Behind Historical Archives, Fontainhas, Panaji, tel: 224966
Dr G K Salelkar, 111, Mahalakshmi Chambers, 18th June Road, Panaji, tel: 42665

Chest Specialists
Netravalkar Nursing Home, Panaji, tel: 221921

Consulting Physician
Dr A A Bandodkar, Sandeep Apartments, Dr Vaidya Road, Panaji, tel: 225257
Dr G K Salelkar, 111, Mahalakshmi Chambers, 18th June Road, Panaji, tel: 42665
Dr Purushottam Caraikar, Peira Alta, Mapusa, tel: 262943

Dentist
Dr (Mrs) Anita S Naik, First Floor, Sincro Towers, Margao, tel: 720827
Dr Gurudas P Mahambre, Cottrarbat, Aldona, tel: 293254
Dr Hubert Gomes, Next to Menaxi Hotel, Reliance Building, Near Cine Blue Pearl, Margao, tel: 722530
Dr (Mrs) Reena Gracias, First Floor, Naina Gracias Building, Near Police] Station, Margao, tel: 720623

Diabetologist
Dr Prakash Prabhu Dessai, A F1 Panchratna Complex,
Martires Dias Road, Margao, tel: 720366

ENT Specialists
Dr Sandeep S Sanzgiri, Opposite High Court, M G Road,
Panaji, tel: 220773
Dr Vivek Sardesai, Mahalaxmmi Chambers, 18th June
Road, Panaji, tel: 225416
Dr Jorson Fernandes, A F1 Panchratna Complex, Martires
Dias Road, Margao, tel: 220366

Opticians
Dr C Liola Pereira, 211, Gracious Building, Near Loyala
High School, Margao, tel: 731627
Dr Sielda Gomes E Souza, D-F 12 Pancharatna, Martins
Dias Road, Margao, tel: 720144
Dr Vivek A Naik Padre, Miranda Road, Margao, tel: 722563
Dr Alka V Prabhu Desai, Shabana Chambers, Panaji,
tel: 225699
Dr Prakash Kuncolienkar, 15 Trionora Apartments,
Opposite El Dorado Cinema, Panaji, tel: 227091
Dr Ulhas Kaisare, A B Road, Panaji, tel: 224317

DRINKS
India has a large variety of both alcoholic and non-
alcoholic drinks. We have listed a few of the more popular
drinks you can sample around in Goa.

Beer
Indian beers have delightful names like Golden Eagle, Rosy
Pelican, Cannon Extra, Bullet, Black Label, Knock Out,
Kingfisher, Guru, Punjab or Kings. They are best drunk
chilled. The most common, Kingfisher, is very weak in
comparison to European beer. Beer and other Indian
interpretations of Western alcoholic drinks are known as
IMFL (Indian Made Foreign Liquor). Rum, gin, whisky,
vodka — almost all alcoholic drinks are available. Indian

rum is surprisingly good, but no white variety is available. Like all spirits in Goa, it is measured in 'fingers'; one finger approximately equals an English triple. Lovers of English gin and Scotch whiskey should make their duty-free supplies last as long as possible, as local versions are rather different. Wine, surprisingly, is also available, manufactured from grapes grown in Hyderabad and Bangalore. The 'dry' white is not too bad, if well chilled, but the red porto is a poor imitation of Portuguese port, having a strangely caramelized flavour.

Feni
A distilled liquor produced from fermented cashew apples or from fermented coconut today. The two varieties taste quite different, the former being stronger (see FENI, page 72).

Juices
The easiest way to buy this is in small cardboard boxes of mango, lemon or apple juice, each sold with a straw. Fresh tender coconut water is popular as are soda water and *lassi*, a refreshing curd (yoghurt) drink.

Soft Drinks
Soft drinks are a safe substitute for water although they tend to have a high sugar content. Coca Cola was asked to leave India a few years ago for not cooperating with the government but is back again under the new liberalised economy of India. Pepsi too has a market here. There are similar indigenous brands like Campa Cola or Thums Up. Limca, Gold Spot, Sprint and others provide versions of lemonade and orangeade.

Tea
Surprisingly, tea is not the all purpose and all important drink it is in Britain and Arab countries. Indians prefer a strong brew with plenty of milk and sugar boiled together. Known as *chai*, some people like it while others try to avoid it. Tea, more to international taste, can be obtained

if you ask for 'Tray Tea', which gives you the tea, milk
and sugar separately. Tea is more popular in the north,
while in the south, coffee is the number one drink.

Toddy A mildly alchoholic extract from the coconut palm
flower (see FENI, page 72)

DRIVING

Driving in Goa is on the left hand side of the road, the
same as in Britain. Drivers need a valid international
driving license or an Indian driving license.

DRUGS

Peddling as well as use of narcotic drugs is an offence
under the Indian Penal Code and is punishable by law
with a maximum punishment of life imprisonment. This
law is strictly implemented by the police in Goa. Most of
the 160 inmates in Aguada Jail, 12 of them foreigners, are
there on drug-related offences.

Despite all this, the dreaded weed is still available in
Goa (it's usually from Kerala). Travellers who have come
from Kashmir or the Kullu Valley may offer you resin but
the quality varies.

DUTY FREE

Duty free allowances in Goa apply to all guests over the
age of 17 years:

Cigarettes and Tobacco: 200 cigarettes or 50 cigars or
250 grams of tobacco
Spirits, wine and liquor: 1 litre spirit or 2 litres of wine
or 2 litres of fortified wine or liquor
Perfumes and gifts: 60 ml of perfume and gifts to the
value of 36.00 pounds sterling.

Please note you will not be able to spend rupees
outside of India.

Leaving Goa:
For UK customs India is classed as a developing country
so no duty is payable on any handicrafts, from baskets
and silks to leather jackets and pottery. VAT, however, is
payable if the total value is more than £136 per person,
and this includes any Middle East airport shopping.

E

ECOLOGY

Goa's largest industry, mining, is a major ecological
concern as it is believed to have damaged paddy fields,
polluted waterways and beaches, as well as accelerated
deforestation. Like elsewhere in the country, when
deforestation takes place, teak, eucalyptus and casuarina
are planted instead of native trees. Industry has also
caused water and air pollution, affecting the vital fish
industry in the rivers, estuaries and sea.

The lesser enemy is tourism whose demands have led
to developments along the coastline, threatening the
pioneer vegetation of salt-tolerant creepers, pandanas and
special spreading cashew trees, not to be confused with
cashewnut producing trees. In 1991, planning regulations
prevented hotels from building above a certain height and
at a 200-metre distance from the high tide line. However,
this has not been properly enforced and fishing villages,
seaside coconut palms and vegetation have vanished,
putting the fragile shoreline ecosystem at risk.

The Konkan Railway, currently under construction, is
another grave concern. Though necessary for the area's
development, it will increase urbanisation and pollution,
destroy the environment and existing birdlife.

For more on Goa's environment, see *Fish, Curry
and Rice : A Citizen's Report on the Goan Environment*
(Rs 200), available at most bookshops.

ELECTRICITY AND VOLTAGE

The electric voltage in India is 220 volts AC, 50 cycles. A continental adaptor transfers three-pin square plugs to the two or three round ones used in India.

Electricity breakdowns and blackouts are not uncommon, so check if your hotel has put a candle and matches in your room. Carrying a torch will be useful.

EMERGENCY CONTACTS (telephone numbers)

Ambulance: 102 all over Goa
Panaji: 224066

Fire Brigade: 101 all over Goa
Panaji: 225500; Margao: 220168; Mapusa: 262900;
Ponda: 312044; Vasco: 513840

Foreigners Regional Registration Office
Police Headquartes, Azad Maidan, Panaji

Hospitals
Goa Medical College Hospital, Panaji: 223658/225727/224566
Asilo Hospital, Mapusa: 262372/262211
Hospicio Hospital, Margao: 722164

Police: 100 all over Goa
Panaji: 223400; Margao: 222175; Mapusa: 262231; Vasco: 512304; Calangute: 278284; Colva: 221254; Canacona: 643357

ETIQUETTE AND CUSTOMS

The traditional form of greeting is the *namaste*, with hands neatly folded together in a prayer-like gesture. However, handshakes are now common.

Incredibly hospitable, Goans are easily offended if refused. Even unexpected visitors will be invited to share in a meal. In many homes, footwear is left just inside the front door to keep out the dirt of the street. However, socks may be kept on. The same applies while visiting a temple. Footwear and any other leather product like belts, bags or wallets are also not allowed inside a temple.

Some special functions call for use of the banana leaf plate and you will have to sit cross-legged on the floor. Sit as comfortably as you can because you will have to eat with your fingers. Use your right hand only, even if you are a south paw. It is considered unclean to use the left hand. Similarly, never give or receive anything with your left hand.

Begging and giving of alms is a religious obligation for most Indians but restrain yourself and do not encourage this practice.

EXCURSIONS
There are many excursion operators. Four good trips to take are:

Crocodile Dundee
This excursion sets off from Vainguinim Beach in front of Hotel Cidade de Goa, where Hydro Sports use traditional dug out canoes (normally used for fishing) shaded by paca fronds. The motorised canoes wend their way through creeks supporting lush mango trees on either side. The quest is on to locate the largest reptiles remaining on earth since the days of the dinosaur! A slither, a break in the water and it's gone — move on — looking for the next basking beast. Lunch is served on a small Goan farm. The meal is cooked by the farmer's wife. The trip continues to Old Goa or returns to the beach.

Spice Plantation
Have you heard of a cashew apple? Did you know that the husk of a cashewnut is used for tanning? This trip stops first at the cashew factory to see how the burning, shelling, cleaning, salting and bagging are done.

Next it stops at a fascinating Hindu temple. Lunch is at the spice plantation set amongst densely populated flora. Afterwards there is an interesting guided tour of the plantation to see herbs, spices, fruit and vegetables growing in their natural habitat — plus a 'Tarzan'-style display of high tree jumping.

A varied and interesting day.

Sunset Cruise

'You fill up my senses, like a sleepy blue ocean.....'
A late afternoon cruise fron Panaji is relaxing. Cocktails in hand, you cruise down the Mandovi River towards the twilight zone of the Arabian Sea to experience the glorious sunset. Music and folk dances fill the return journey with a stop at a local restaurant to complete the evening.

Tiracol Fort

An almost indescribable day. If you do nothing else in Goa, this one excursion is the 'Star of India.'

Drive north taking in stunning scenery — stopping every 20 minutes or so, watch climbers shinning up coconut palms, or taste freshly cut coconuts, or view a local distillery and taste its potent product, or see potters making their terracotta dishes.

You can enjoy the kaleidoscope of green lushness, the simple ferries, Goa's more remote beaches, a picnic lunch and, finally, Tiracol Fort, captured by the Portuguese during the 16th century and used by them to guard the northernmost tip of Goa.

A superb day out which should not be missed — young or old.

F

FENI

The coconut palm and cashew tree are abundant in Goa and produce a drink unique to the state — *feni* (or froth in Konkani, referring to the fermenting action). The art of distillation was introduced by the Portuguese missionaries, who also brought the cashew tree to Goa from Brazil.

Festivals are celebrated with colour, processions and folk dances.

Carnival celebrations.

Feast of Three Kings, Reis Magos.

Goa's mansions contain vestiges of a colonial past.

Elements of Goan architecture.

The production of *feni* remains at the level of a cottage industry. For coconut *feni*, licensed toddy-tappers collect the sap of the young shoots at the top of tree, whereas the extracted juice of the ripe cashew fruit is fermented to make *caju* (cashew) *feni*. The first distillation produces the milder *urrack*.

Feni is generally purchased from traverns. Coconut *feni* tastes slightly of coconut, but the flavour of *caju feni* is hard to describe. All these spirits can be drunk neat or mixed with freshly-squeezed lime juice or with the regular brands of soft drinks. If purchasing a bottle of *feni* to take home, ensure that it is adequately sealed.

FERRIES
Goa is dominated by a complex system of waterways formed by the various rivers and their tributaries that drain down from the Western Ghats into the Arabian Sea. Very few of these rivers have bridges across them, so people depend on the local ferry service.

Useful services include:
Ribander to Chorao; Old Goa to Divar; Vanxim to Old Goa; Vanxim to Itagem (Divar); Naroa to Divar; Volvoi to Surla Maina; Aldona to Corjuem; Panaji to Betim; Amona to Khandola; Pomburpa to Chorao; Aronda to Kiranpani; Raia to Siroda; Assolna to Cavelossim; Carona to Calvim; Sarmanos to Tonca; Cortalim to Marcaim; Savoi Verem to Tishem; Dhurbat to Rassoi; Kothambi Keri to Tiracol; Siolim to Chopdem.
The smaller rivers can be crossed by a canoe.
There is also a launch service from Dona Paula jetty to the Mormugao Harbour (September to May).

FESTIVALS AND PUBLIC HOLIDAYS
Goa has an astonishing number of festivals, partly because it celebrates the local and national ones of all religions. Public holidays are those recognised throughout India

when all shops, banks and business close, whatever be the religion of the owners and workers.

Hindu festivals tend to follow the lunar calendar and are usually very colourful. Many celebrate a natural event such as the advent of spring, the success of the harvest season or instruments of farm work. Some are celebrated with Marathi plays and bull fights.

The native Christians of Goa are mainly Roman Catholic. Almost every village in Goa has its own village church which is dedicated to at least one saint. This means that all these churches celebrate at least one feast every year. Goans, the fun loving people, celebrate their feasts with great pomp, vigour and revelry. They usually hold a village dance or organise a *tiatro*, or sport events such as football and cricket matches or a bull fight and have a small village fair.

Muslim festivals move right round the year. Thus, Ramzaan or Ramadan (30 days of fasting during the ninth month of the Muslim calendar), Id-ul-Fitr (celebrating the end of Ramzaan), Id-ul-Zuha (remembering Abraham's attempted sacrifice of Ishmail) and Muharram (ten days of mourning for the murder in AD 680 of the Prophet Mohammad's grandson) will be celebrated at different times each year by Goa's small Muslim population; the exception is the *Urs* (death anniversary) on 17 February. The best place to see the pomp of the two Id festivals is Safa Masjid, just outside Ponda.

The date on which a festival falls differs from year to year. To know the exact date, consult a local calendar.

January

The Feast of the Three Kings (6th), Christian. Celebrated with great pomp and show in the villages of Reis Magos, named after the Three Wise Men, in Bardez.

Jatra, Hindu. The Jatra is the feast of the god to whom the temple is dedicated. Best at Shantadurga Temple at Fatorpa in Quepem, at Bogdgeshwar Temple in Mapusa and Devki Krishna Ravalnath Temple at Marcela in Ponda. This festival is also celebrated in other temples of importance.

Republic Day (26th), national. Celebrates India's establishment as a republic in 1950. A spectacular show takes place in New Delhi where there is a colourful and impressive military parade, but celebrations take place throughout the country. Schoolchildren march past and a cultural show is the norm once the national flag is hoisted.

February

Feast of Our Lady of Candelaria (2nd), Christian. A popular feast celebrated at Pomburpa's church.

Carnival (the week before Lent), Christian. A three-day riot of fun and colour preludes 40 days of penance and total abstinence. There are processions of sponsored floats, tableaux and clowns. People from all over the country come to enjoy the big celebrations held in Panaji, Margao, Mapusa and Vasco. Carnival ends with the Red and Black Dance, held on Ash Wednesday at Clube Nacional, Panaji, when partygoers dress in red and black.

Urs of Shah Abdullah (17th), Muslim. Death-anniversary of this saint, when there may be a chance to hear *quawwalis*, the lyrical Muslim devotional songs, often sung through the night, at Ponda.

Vasant Panchami Jatra, Hindu. Best at Shantadurga Temple at Queula, near Ponda; other *vasant* (spring) festivals at all temples but especially at Mangesh Temple, Priol, and at Mahalsa Temple, Mardol, both in Ponda, at Ajoba Temple at Querim in Pernem and at Mahalaxmi Temple at Amone in Bicholim.

March

Mahashivratri Jatra, Hindu. Best at Siroda and Ramnath both in Ponda and at Sanguem; also good at Harvalem, Kavlem and Mangesh temples. This festival celebrates the birth of Lord Shiva.

Shigmotsav, Hindu. Shigmo, like Holi elsewhere, is the spring festival of colour celebrated on the full moon day of the month of *Phalgun* (generally in March). There is a procession of floats at Panaji, Mapusa, Vasco da Gama and Margao. Everybody can join in the singing and dancing. Sweets are distributed and old grudges are forgotten. At times the celebration might turn rowdy.

April

Easter Week, Christian. Celebrations in most churches on Palm Sunday (Sunday before Easter), Maunday Thursday, Good Friday (mass at 11 pm) and Easter Day.

Procession of All Saints of the Franciscan Third Order (Monday following Palm Sunday), Christian. This procession from St Andrew's Church through Goa Velha on the 5th Sunday in Lent also takes place in Rome but nowhere else in the world. More than 20 figures of saints grandly parade around the streets on decorated floats.

The Feast of Jesus of Nazareth (1st Sunday after Easter), Christian. Celebrated at Sirigao church.

Feast of Our Lady of Miracles (16 days after Easter), Christian. Celebrated in Mapusa's church.

Mahavir Jayanti, Jain. The main festival celebrated by the strictly vegetarian Jain community. Marks the birth of Mahavir, the founder of Jainism, and is a public holiday. Best at Borim in Ponda.

Ramanavami Jatra, Hindu. Marks the birth of Lord Rama, a reincarnation of the god Vishnu. Best at Partagal in Canacona.

May

Goa Statehood Day (30th), state. State holiday to celebrate Goa becoming the 25th state of the Indian Union on 30 May 1987.

June

Feast of St Anthony (13th), Christian. Throughout Goa, the saint is entreated to bring rain; Hindus meanwhile, perform their rain *pujas*.

Feast of St John (20th), Christian. Throughout Goa, young men beg freshly distilled *feni* from their neighbours and then jump into village wells.

August
Independence Day (15th), national. Commemorates India's independence from British rule. A solemn ceremony in a public ground where a political leader hoists the national flag and gives a speech.

Feast of St Lawrence, Christian. Celebrates the end of the monsoon and the re-opening of the sand bar that annually silts up the Mandovi River.

Gokul Ashtami, Hindu. Krishna's birthday, across Goa; marks the beginning of the harvest season.

Festival of Novidades (24th), state. The first sheaves of the rice crop are offered to the chief minister. The harvest festival is celebrated in churches. The priest gathers the first rice from the fields and returns to the church, accompanied by music and fireworks, blesses it and distributes it among the congregation. After this, the harvesting begins in earnest.

September
Ganesh/Ganapati Chaturthi, Hindu. One of the most popular Hindu festivals, celebrates the elephant-headed Hindu god of good fortune and prosperity, Ganesh or Ganapati. Each Hindu family or community keeps a statue of Ganesh in their home or temple for a period of one to 11 days. The statue is then paraded through the streets and eventually immersed in the nearby river or sea.

October
Gandhi Jayanti (2nd), national. Celebrates the birth of Mahatma Gandhi. Prayer meetings are held at the memorial site in Delhi. As a sign of respect it is a Dry Day (no alcohol is served). Gandhi, through whose non-violent revolt India gained Independence from British rule is the most revered of all Indian leaders ever.

Dussehra/Dharotsav, Hindu. This extremely popular ten-day long Hindu festival begins on the first day of the Hindu month of *Ashvina*. The festival celebrates the triumph of good over evil and culminates in the burning of the effigy of the demon king, Ravana. In Goa, the main *puja* of this festival is performed at the place of work. Machinery, tool, vehicles, etc, are cleaned and garlanded with flowers and worshipped.

Fama de Menino Jesus (3rd Sunday in October), Christian. The festival of little Jesus, celebrated at Colva.

November

Diwali, Hindu. Celebrated on the 15th day of the Hindu month *Kartika* (early to mid-November), celebrates the return of Lord Rama from exile in south India to his home at Ayodhya in the north. In the evening thousands of oil lamps are lit on each rooftop to show him the way and welcome him back. The festival lasts five days with ceremonies each day. Friends and family give each other sweets. Best at Mandrem in Pernem, at Vithal Temple in Margao, at Naguesh Temple and Marcaim Temple in Ponda.

Feast of Our Lady of the Rosary (3rd Wednesday of November), Christian. Celebrated in Navelim's church.

December

Feast of St Francis Xavier (3rd), Christian. The feast of the patron saint of Goa is celebrated on the day he died in 1552. Preceding the feast, nine days of Novenas are held, attended by pilgrims from all over the world. Stalls selling sweetmeats, toys, clothing, etc, line the streets.

Feast of Our Lady of the Immaculate Conception, Christian. Celebrated in December in the churches of Panaji and Margao. Panaji has a street fair forming an arcade over the roads.

Christmas Day (25th), Christian. Christmas is celebrated throughout India, but most notably in Goa. The

25th of December is the main feast of the year for Goans. After midnight mass, people flock out of their local churches for the village dances. This is the season for sending and receiving greetings, exchanging sweets and gifts, and singing carols. There are Star and Crib competitions and carol singing competitions. This festive season continues until the 6th of January. Each night there are hundreds of beach parties and roadside bands encourage every passerby to join in the celebration.

New Year's Eve (31st). Jubilant celebrations, in the form of all-night street parties and beach parties anticipate the good things the New Year will bring.

FOOD (see CUISINE, page 61)

Goa is predominantly agricultural. A major part of its population lives in villages rather than towns. There are only four large towns in Goa and seven smaller ones, while the remaining area consists of villages.

Agricultural methods are slowly improving. The old methods of ploughing, sowing, farming and harvesting are slowly being discarded for modern equipment. Manure consisting of ash, decomposed fish and cowdung are now being replaced with artificial fertilisers.

Rice is the chief crop. There are three varieties — *sorod*, *vaingan* and *morod*. *Sorod* is grown during the rainy season, while the *vaingan* is grown in summer using irrigation. *Morod* is also grown during the monsoon but mainly confined to hilly and mountainous tracts.

Cereals such as *nachino* (ragi), *pakad* and *vary* are grown on a large scale as they do not require as much moisture as rice. They are grown on the hill slopes and in drier parts. Pulses such as *alsando* and *urad* (blackgram) are also cultivated.

Sugarcane, being a tropical plant, grows well especially around Sanguem, Colem and Rivona. Sweet potatoes are grown in summer chiefly at Agacaim.

Onions and lady's fingers are mainly cultivated in the

lowlands. Chillies are grown in summer all over the territory. Areca-palms are mostly found at Ponda, Canacona, Sanguem and Quepem. The leaves of the betel vine, a thin long creeper which grows up the areca-palms' trunk, are chewed as a digestive called *paan*.

FORTS

Goa's forts may not have the dramatic quality of those built by the Mughals and Rajputs in north India. But they are interesting all the same. When the Portuguese occupied Goa they built a series of fortresses along the coast to protect their domains using Italian engineering techniques of low, thick, sloping walls, wide moats and cylindrical turrets.

Chapora Fort (1717), at the northern end of Bardez's coastline, dominates the landscape. The Portuguese built the great laterite walls with their cupola-topped turrets large enough to accommodate the local population against Maratha attack. Little to see, though the views from the ramparts are magnificent.

Fort Aguada (1612), situated high on the cliffs to defend Aguada Bay and the mouth of River Mandovi, was by far the most invincible of Goa's forts, equipped with 79 cannons strategically placed on the ramparts, ready to attack. Its most important sights are the old lighthouse, built in 1846, and the charming Church of St Lawrence, patron saint of sailors, built in 1630. The main citadel is now a prison.

Tiracol Fort (18th century) was occupied by the Portuguese in 1746. Earlier it was the stronghold of a local raja. It was the base for freedom fighters during the liberation of Goa in 1961. Within the fort is the small Church of St Anthony

FRUITS (see FOOD, page 87)

If your sweet tooth is simply not sweet enough to cope with too many Indian desserts, you'll be able to fall back on India's wide variety of fruit. It varies from tropical delights in the south to apricots and other temperate-region fruits in the north. Specialities include cherries and strawberries in Kashmir; apricots in Ladakh and Himachal Pradesh.

In Goa, melons are widespread, particularly watermelons, which are found in sandy areas, only in summer and are a fine thirst–quencher.

The coconut palm flourishes in abundance in Goa, where the soil is salty and sandy. Each and every part is used. The ripe coconut is used for cooking. The juice of the tender coconut is used as a refreshment. The fronds are matted and used as a shade for the house to protect the occupants from the summer heat. It is also used to extract *toddy* to make *feni*. There are coconut stalls on many street corners. When you have drunk the tender coconut water, the stall-holder will split the coconut open and cut you a slice from the outer coverings to use to scoop the flesh out.

A huge variety of bananas are grown in India, particularly in the south, as well as two varieties of jackfruits. These as well as papaya and plantain trees are visible in most gardens. Pineapples are grown commercially.

The cashew is a summer fruit found mainly in the hilly regions. Its season lasts for about three to four months. When the juice from the cashew fruit is fermented and distilled, the first distillation is called *urrack*, which is very low in alcohol content. Subsequent distillations yield cashew *feni* which has a strong flavour, a smoky taste and is very potent. The nuts are used in cooking and for making sweets.

Many varieties of mangoes are found in Goa. Some of them are Malcorada, Fernandina, Alfonso, Colaco and Monserrate. Each variety has its own peculiar taste and flavour. Green mangoes are preserved in water and spices and called *chepni* and *miscut*.

G

GOVERNMENT

Goa has 40 legislators in the Goa State Legislative Assembly and is represented nationally in New Delhi by two elected members in the Lok Sabha and one nominated to the Rajya Sabha (the two houses of the Indian Parliament). The Governor is the Head of the State and is advised by a Council of Ministers, headed by the Chief Minister.

GUIDES

Trained guides are available on request from the Government of India Tourist Officer at the Communidade Building, Church Square, Panaji, tel: 43412.

H

HAIRDRESSERS

Almost all de-luxe hotels have a hairdresser on the premises, which are open to non-residents as well. Beauty parlours and barber shops are located in most shopping areas and markets too.

HEALTH

Before leaving the UK, it is wise to consult a doctor about vaccinations and inoculations. However, while in Goa, there are a few extra precautions you can take to protect yourself.

   Malaria Tablets : As these have been known to cause mild stomach irritations, it is better to take them after a meal. The once-a-week tablets should be taken after the evening meal.

   Dehydration : The most common health problem in Goa, this can make you feel very weak and listless. The first symptoms are feeling weak, tired and drained. To avoid them, drink lots and lots of fluid, especially bottled water. When eating snacks and meals always add a little extra salt than usual, as this retains the water in your system — thus decreasing the chances of dehydration. As a guide, where you would normally drink one glass of water, drink three.

Stomach upsets : Avoid them by keeping well hydrated. But if one strikes, drink lots of fluid (water with a little salt and sugar). If possible starve your system for 24 hours. But if not, stick to plain boiled rice with salt and a squeeze of lemon. If you are diabetic or have a fever as well, contact a doctor immediately. Avoid the sun in all situations of ill health.

HOLIDAYS (see FESTIVALS, page 81)

HOSPITALS (see EMERGENCY CONTACTS, page 70)
In addition to the government hospitals, there are a number of private hospitals and nursing homes all over the state.

I

INSURANCE
Travel insurance is one of the most important elements of your holiday. Bring a copy of your travel insurance policy with your other documents. Keep this safe with your passport and flight tickets. A policy will be of use to you in the following circumstances:

- Loss of property (articles or money)
- Medical cost incurred while overseas
- Personal liability
- Personal accident

K

KONKANI
Konkani is the Goan local language. Though it is an independent language in its own right, Konkani is similar

to **Hindi** and **Marathi**, the language of neighbouring Maharashtra. Also, though the official script of the language is Devnagari, people of different religions, and from different areas write Konkani in different scripts. The Christian Goanese normally writes Konkani in the Roman script, but their writing follows Portuguese models and is mixed with Portuguese expressions. The Hindus use the Devnagari script to write Konkani and speak the Konkani recognised by the Sahitya Academy. Besides these, **Kannada** and **Malayalam** scripts are also in use depending on different circumstances.

Before the liberation of Goa, the upper class Christians conducted all affairs in **Portuguese**. However, most Goans, also, understand and speak **English** quite well. In fact it has replaced Portuguese among many of the upper crust families though, even today you will find quite a few people conversing in Portuguese.

The national language of India, **Hindi**, is quite readily accepted here as well.

A simple survival vocabulary is:

English	Konkani	English	Konkani
Yes	*Voi*	One	*Ek*
No	*Na*	Two	*Dhon*
Thank you	*Dayo bor-ray koru*	Three	*Teen*
Sorry	*Suk zali*	Four	*Char*
It's a warm day	*Eyes gorom zata*	Five	*Parnts*
Cheers!	*Viva!*	Six	*So*
How are you?	*Two kosso assai* (man)	Seven	*Sat*
	Two kossi assai (woman)		
I'm fine	*Bor-ray ha*	Eight	*Art*
I don't want	*Maka naka*	Nine	*Nov*
Not spicy please	*Maka teak naka*	Ten	*Dua*
I love you	*Ow two-zo mog kotta*		

L

LANGUAGE

The languages of India form part of its complexity. The country's political and regional boundaries are drawn on linguistic lines.

There is no 'Indian' language, which is part of the reason why English is widely spoken by about 20 percent of the population. **Hindi** and **English** are the national languages of India. Hindi is predominant in the north — and also related to other northern languages such as Urdu, Punjabi, Gujarati, Oriya and Bangla — it bears little relation to the Dravidian languages of the south where very few people speak Hindi. Tamil is the most important Dravidian language (while others include Telugu, Kannada and Malayalam) and English, not Hindi, is the connecting language and often the first language of the educated. Thus, for visitors it is very easy to get around India with English. Nevertheless, it is always nice to know at least a little of the local language.

LAUNDRY

Most hotels have their own laundry service, or have arrangements to provide this service to the hotel guests.

LOSS/THEFT

In case of loss or theft at your hotel premises, first contact the person in charge (usually the Front Office Manager). It is also necessary to make a formal police complaint at the local police station and to have a photocopy of your complaint if you intend to make an insurance claim.

M

MARKETS

Flea Market, Anjuna: The village of Anjuna throbs with life every Wednesday when the weekly flea market is held on the beach. By mid–morning it gets crowded and by 11 am there is not even space to walk.

Several narrow paths lead to a shady coconut grove just before the sand. It is a riot of colour, people of different nationalities speaking different languages and a vast variety of wares and sounds — Kashmiri and Tibetan traders, colourful Gujarati tribal women and carefree Western travellers and hippies sell whatever you need, from used paperbacks to a new swimsuit. Bargain hard to get a reasonable deal.

You can spend the whole day just browsing or relaxing under the shade of a coconut palm. Refreshment stalls and small restaurants do brisk business.

By late afternoon the crowd lessens, traffic gets thinner, and as the sun sets, it's time to pack up and leave.

Mapusa Market: A famous open air market, held every Friday. Its origins date back to the 15th century, making it one of the oldest markets in Goa. Today, there is a strong tourist element. However, local produce is displayed; potted plants, vegetables, giant Moira bananas, chillies from the tiny *put-ki-pari* or *malagetta* to the almost black *calvim* variety, spices, pottery, bamboo mats and baskets, rope, coconut shell ladles and almost everything is sold here. Another speciality of the market are the cross-strapped, hand-stitched leather sandals on sale.

The surrounding shops sell gold and silver jewellery, silk and cotton fabric. There is a municipal shed at the back of the market where vendors sell dry fish and seafood, vinegar, flowers, coconut jaggery, Goan sweets and cakes.

Margao: Goa's most interesting daily markets are clustered together in the town centre: the fresh fish market, the fruit and vegetable market and the huge covered market where everything from chillies and nuts to household goods are sold. This is a market used by locals, full of interest, with no tourists.

MEASUREMENT SYSTEM
In Goa, as in the rest of India, the metric system is followed.

MOTORBIKES
Very popular and the fastest and most economic way of getting about.

An unique feature of Goa are the motorcycle taxis or 'motorcycle pilots'. They are easily recognised by the yellow guards and white number plates and can carry only one pillion rider at a time. They ply between towns and within them, and have special taxi stands of their own. One can even hire a motorbike for oneself, quite easily. The bikes available are Enfield India, a replica of the old British Royal Enfield Bullet, as well as newer Japanese designed 100 cc models. There are also gearless Kinetic Honda scooters. The cost of hiring a bike for the day is Rs200 to Rs400. The local beach boys can easily arrange one for you. To hire a bike you will probably have to deposit your passport or make a substantial down payment as security money.

MUSEUMS
Archaeological Museum and Potrait Gallery, Old Goa (tel: 286133). This museum, founded in 1964, is housed in the abandoned convent of St Francis of Assisi at Old Goa. Its collection includes Brahmanical sculptures, portraits of Portuguese grandees such as Vasco da Gama, Joao de Crasto and Bernado Peres da Silva and a large bronze statue of Alfonso de Albuquerque. There is a model of a 16th-century Portuguese ship and a collection of Indo-Portuguese coins. The most important exhibit is the centrally positioned Hindu carving of Vishnu believed to be a thousand years old.
Open: Daily except Fridays; 10 am to 12 noon and 1 to 5 pm. No entrance fee is charged.

While you are there you can also visit the galleries at **Se Cathedral** and the **Basilica of Bom Jesus**. Open: Daily; 9 am to 12.30 pm and 3 to 6.30 pm.

Menezes Braganza Institute, Panaji (tel: 224143).
Originally called Instituto Vasco da Gama, this institute
was founded by the poet, Thomas Rebeiro, to facilitate the
study of arts and science in Goa on 22 November 1871. It
is situated on Malacca Road, opposite Azad Maidan in
Panaji. It has rare paintings, sculptures, numismatic and
philatelic collections. The walls of the entrance are
beautifully covered with blue Portuguese ceramic tiles
called *azulejos*, hand painted by Jorge Colace. The
paintings depict passages from the *Os Lusiadas*, a
Portuguese epic written by Luis de Camoes. The building
also houses Goa's Central Library which has a large
collection of rare books and documents.
Open: Monday to Friday; 9.30 am to 5.30 pm.

Monastery of Pilar, Goa Velha (tel: 8549). The monastery
is situated on Pilar Hill, Goa Velha (NH 17). It has a small
museum containing relics of pre-historic Goa, and the
Kadamba period. The seminary is one of the two surviving
theological colleges founded by the Portuguese.
Open: Daily; 9 am to 5 pm.

Museum of the Archives of Goa, Panaji (tel: 46006).
Located at Ashirwad Building, 1st floor, St Inez, Panaji,
this museum's mostly pre-colonial collections include
sculptures, coats-of-arms, paintings, coins, manuscripts,
woodwork, etc. The inscriptions of Goan history dating
back to the fourth century AD, indicating that the Bhojas,
Mauryas, Shilaharas and Kadambas were the dynasties
ruling Goa in the past, are also seen here.
Open: Tuesday to Friday and Sunday; 9.30 am to 1 pm
and 2 to 5.30 pm. Closed on Saturdays, Mondays and
public holidays.

Museum of Christian Art, Rachol. This museum,
adjoining Rachol Church, is perhaps the only place where
one can see Portuguese art tinted with Indian influence. It
also has a wide array of crucifixes, goblets, crowns,

chalices, staffs, etc. The seminary here is the biggest in Asia.

Open: Daily except Mondays; 9.30 am to 5.30 pm. There is an entrance fee of Rs5 for adults and Rs2 for children.

N

NEWSPAPERS

Several newspapers are available in Goa. There are Goa's own newspapers in English and Marathi, and the national newspapers which reach Goa from Mumbai. English dailies published in Goa include: *Navhind Times, Herald* and *Gomantak Times,* which also publishes a newspaper in Marathi.

NIGHTLIFE

Goans are music lovers and play Western as well as Indian music. From October to May, dances are organised at various clubs, streets and on the beach. Almost every village church feast is followed by a dance. The most popular feasts are Christmas, New Year's Eve, Easter and Carnival, when the whole of Goa seems to be celebrating.

Besides these, there is a growing number of discotheques, some of which are in hotels. Others, like The Mad Cat Club in Cavelossim and Lido in Dona Paula are equally popular. The Cidade de Goa has recently opened the innovative Beachoteque. Further up north there is Tito's Bar. An evening of live music, cultural entertainment and dance can also be enjoyed at the Alva Mar at Parra, near Mapusa, and at the Kerkar Art Gallery at Calangute. The casinos at the Goa Renaissance Hotel and the Cidade de Goa are there for those who would like to try their luck.

NUDISM

Nudism is not permitted on the beaches of Goa, and is punishable by law.

P

PASSPORT

All overseas travellers are required to carry a valid passport of their country when entering India. It is wise to keep it in a hotel locker, and never to take it to the beach.

PHARMACY

The four main towns are well supplied. Many are noted in Goan newspapers. The major pharmacies in Panaji are:
Hindu Pharmacy, opposite Municipal Garden Square
Pharmacia Menezes, near the Main Post Office
Chandu Pharmacies, near Municipal Market
Pharmacia Salcete, near the Panaji Circle

For those in search of **homeopathic**, **allopathic**, and **ayurvedic** drugs and medication, the **Hindu Pharmacy** is the only pharmacy in the state which possesses a good stock.

The government has made it compulsory for at least one pharmacy in every city to be open at night in case of emergencies. The **all night** pharmacies in Goa are :
Universal Pharmacy, Fontainhas, Panaji; **Balu Pharmacy**, Aquem-Margao; **Holy Spirit Pharmacy**, Margao, and **Ramakant Medico**, Vasco.

PHOTOGRAPHY

The following stock a wide variety of camera films for slides. Be sure to check the expiry date.

Calangute
Mangesh Photo Studio, 7 Benson Complex Market

Mapusa
Remy Photo Studio, Opposite Dena Bank

Margao
Antao Photographers, Near Cine Lata
Fotocare, 77 Govind Cemba
Golden Needle, Kepem Road

Lorenz and Sons, Behind the Municipality Building
Maujo Photo Studio, Near Municipality Building
Wander Colour Lab, 8 Garden View Apartments

Panaji
Kishore Korart, 5 Diamond Chambers, 18th June Road
Konica Square, Durga Chambers, 18th June Road
Konica Square, Mahalaxmi Chambers, 18th June Road
Super Art, Souza Towers, Opposite Municipal Gardens
Warner and Sons, Behind the Municipality
Lazos, 7 Gharse Towers, Albuquerque Road
National Colour Lab, 5 Municipality Building, Near Cine
El Dorado

POLICE (see EMERGENCY CONTACTS, page 70)

There are several kinds of police in Goa. The most
common are the Traffic Police. Traffic rules are strict, and
if you are driving a vehicle, the valid documents of the
vehicle, your driving license, and passport (in case of
foreign nationals) have to be in your possession, ready for
inspection. Traffic police are clothed in khaki uniform.

Tourist Police in blue uniform, should be contacted
for general assistance.

A third kind of policeman is concerned with criminal
investigations.

POPULATION

The population of Goa is approximately 14,68,622
(nearly 1.5 million). Literacy is 76.96 percent. Sex ratio is
969/1,000 females/males.

POSTS AND TELEGRAPH

The poste restente at the GPO is efficient. They give you
the whole pile to sort through yourself and willingly
check other pigeon holes if expected letters have not
arrived. Open from 9.30 am to 1 pm and 2 to 5.30 pm,
Monday to Saturday.

International telephone calls are handled at the 24-hour central telegraph office, but it is quicker and only marginally more expensive to use one of the many private ISD/STD booths around town.

R

RAILWAYS
India's vast railway system is being upgraded so it is all broad gauge. Journeys to all parts will be much simpler. Meanwhile the construction of the national project, the Konkan Railway from Mumbai to Mangalore is presently underway. After this is completed, Goa will be connected to the rest of India via broad gauge.

Tickets should always be bought from authorised sales counters. Tickets are available at the railway stations in Margao and Vasco, and the Bus Stand, Panaji. It is best to make advance reservations.

RELIGION
Of the entire population of Goa, roughly one third are Christians (38 percent) and most of the remainder are Hindus, with about two percent Muslims.

RESTAURANTS
Unusually for India, Goa abounds in restaurants of different kinds to suit different tastes and different budgets. Almost every nook and corner seems to have a restaurant ranging from the elegant to the very simple. Most have a license to serve alcohol. Cuisines range from Continental to Chinese to Tandoori and, of course, the local Goan delicacies.

Most hotels in Goa have their own restaurants. In addition there are some favourites:

Alfama, Cidade de Goa, Vainguinim Beach, Dona Paula, tel: 221133

A Lua Hotel, Bhuttem Bhatt, Merces, tel: 228213
Banyan Tree, Taj Holiday Inn, Sinquerim, tel: 276201
Bar-B-Que, Majorda Beach Resort, Majorda, tel: 220751
Barbeque at the Lawns, Cidade de Goa, Vainguinim Beach, Dona Paula, tel: 221133
Beach Bar, Taj Holiday Village, Sinquerim, tel: 276201
Beach Boogie, Hotel Miramar, D B Samadhi Marg, Panaji, tel: 226662
Beach House, Taj Holiday Village, Sinquerim, tel: 276201
Beach Wok, Majorda Beach Resort, Majorda, tel: 220751
Cajueiro, Alto-Betim, Panjim-Mapusa Highway, Porvorim, tel: 217375
Capuccino Bar & Restaurant, Mezzanine, Dr D R D'Souza Road, Panaji, tel: 44693
Cavala, The Sea Side Resort, near Baga Beach, Calangute, tel: 276090
Cegonhas, Paraiso de Praia, Baga-Calangute, tel: 277470
China Town, Near Bus Stand, Calangute
Chung-Wa, Hotel Samrat, Dada Vaidya Road, Panaji, tel: 223318
Club House, Taj Holiday Village, Sinquerim, tel: 276201
Delhi Darbar Restaurant & Bar, Panaji, tel: 222544
Dekhni, Cidade de Goa, Vainguinim Beach, Dona Paula, tel: 221133
Gaffino's Beach Resort, near the beach, Mobor, tel: 246385
Gato Loco, Garth Leisure Beach, Cavelossim, tel: 245052
Goa Corner Bar and Restaurant, Chaudi, Canacona
Goa Woodshade, M L Furtado Road, Hotel Goa Woodlands, Margao, tel: 221121
Grandpa's Inn, Anjuna Road, Anjuna, tel: 273271
Holiday Inn Resort Goa, 101 Mobor Beach, Cavelossim, tel: 246303
Hotel Abhiruchi, Ponda, tel: 312675
Hotel Linda Goa, Baga Road, Calangute, tel: 276066
Hotel Ronil Royale, Baga-Calangute Road, Calangute, tel: 276183
Knock Inn, 423 Casa Esmeralda, Pequeno Peddem, tel: 274325

Lafremich, Captain Lobo's Beach Hideaway, Calangute, tel: 276106

La Gondola, The Leela Beach Resort, Mobor, tel: 246363

Laguna, Majorda Beach Resort, Majorda, tel: 220751

Lazeez Bar & Restaurant, Hotel Summit, Near Fidalgo, Panaji, tel: 46734

La Paz Gardens, Swatantra Path, Vasco

Le Millionaire, Padmavati Towers, 1st Floor, 18th June Road, Panaji

Lobster Pot, near the Beach, Calangute

Marina Resorts Private Limited, Calangute-Baga Road, Calangute, tel: 276155

Mermaid Bar & Restaurant, Swimsea, Dona Paula, Caranzalem Beach, tel: 225422

Miramar, Cidade de Goa, Vainguinim Beach, Dona Paula, tel: 221133

Mississippi Restaurant and Pub, Osborne Resorts, Calangute, tel: 263260

O'Coqueiro Bar and Restaurant, Porvorim, tel: 217271

Ocean Terrace, The Leela Beach Resort, Mobor, tel: 246363

Panjim Inn, 31 January Road, Panaji

Peacock Alley, The Leela Beach Resort, Mobor, tel: 246363

Raisa's Place, Baga-Calangute Road

Resorte Paraiso de Praie, Baga-Calangute Road

Riverside Wharf, The Leela Beach Resort, Mobor, tel: 246363

Roof Garden Bar & Restaurant, Summer Ville, Candolim, tel: 262681

St Francis Xavier Shack, Fort Aguada Beach Resort, Sinquerim, tel: 276201

Sea Lounge & Lobby Bar, The Leela Beach Resort, Mobor, tel: 246363

Sea Shell Restaurant, Fort Aguada Beach Resort, Sinquerim, tel: 276201

Sher-e-Punjab, 18th June Road, Panaji, tel: 228309

Sticky Fingers, Hotel Bismarcks, Vasco, tel: 512277

The Bougainvilla, Grandpa's Inn, Anjuna, tel: 273271

The King's Table, The Citadel, Pe J Vaz Road, Near Municipal Gardens, Vasco, tel: 513190

The Waterfall & Terrace, The Leela Beach Resort, Mobor, tel: 246363
Trattoria, Fort Aguada Beach Resort, Sinquerim, tel: 276201
Venite, 31 January Road, Panaji
Village Bar-Be-Que, Holiday Inn Averina, Mobor Beach, tel: 246303
Village Nook Garden Pub & Eat-Out, Church Street, Alto-Porvorim, tel: 217785

Other Resturants:
Casa Portuguese Bar and Restaurant, Baga
Five Flowers, Majorda
Infantaria Pastry Shop, Calangute
St Anthony's Bar and Restaurant, Baga
Tito's Bar-Restaurant, Calangute-Baga Road
21 Coconuts, Candolim

S

SEA

Goa has a 106-kilometre-long coastline. The shores are rocky or sandy. Most are sandy and good for swimming. It is best to consult the lifeguard on the beach before venturing into the water as at certain places the underground slope is not even and may suddenly drop down steeply. Between the months of March and early October the sea can be quite rough. At all times there can be an undertow which is stronger when the tide is going down.

SHOPPING

Most shops open Monday to Saturday, and close on Sundays and public holidays. The hours they usually keep are 9:30 am to 1 pm and 4 to 7 pm, with a lunchbreak and siesta from 1 to 4 pm.

Most shops accept travellers' cheques, Visa, MasterCard and American Express cards.

Besides the daily local markets in every village, the big weekly markets of Mapusa and Anjuna, and the in-house shops of de-luxe hotels, some good shops are:

Margao
Borkar's Superstore, Food Affair, Marliz Bakery, all stock food products and cater to practical needs

Pacheoco, in the New Market area, has an excellent stock of silk

Romilla, at da Costa Chambers, sells high quality Goan paintings, leather and pottery from Goa, Bengal and Pondicherry

Panaji
Benetton, the landmark European store, has an outlet here and sells Western clothes

Champs has a wide range of sports goods

Government of Goa Handicrafts Emporium (branches in Calangute, Mapusa and Margao), sells items made in Goa like lace, colourful masks, terracotta, cotton bags, wooden toys and table-mats woven from sisal of banana, coconut or pineapple fibre

Mr Baker specialises in delicious cashewnut cakes and macroons

Silk Emporium sells silk as well as provides tailoring services

Sirsat, near the High Court, is a jeweller used by old Goan families

Velhos & Filhos, is a general store with a good stock ranging from sauces and pickles to games and beachballs

Zantyes (branch in Mapusa) is the ultimate cashew shop. (Also see **Cajuwalla** and **U P Traders** for cashewnuts and other dried fruit)

Finally, **Camelot** in Ribandar has the best quality contemporary Indian clothes and household furnishings displayed by Ritu Nanda in her old riverside home (House no 139, Fondrem, Ribandar. Tel: (0832) 234255.

Along River Mandovi.

PANAJI (Panjim)

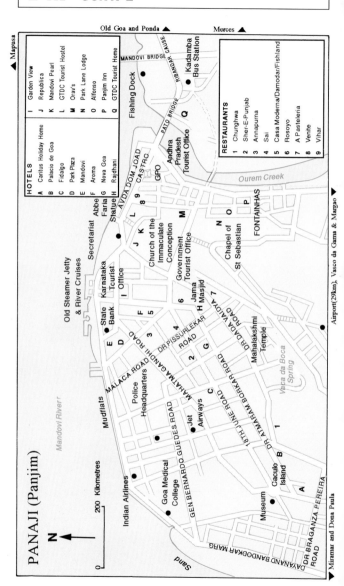

HOTELS

A	Caritus Holiday Home
B	Palacio de Goa
C	Fidalgo
D	Park Plaza
E	Mandovi
F	Aroma
G	Nova Goa
H	Rajdhani
I	Garden View
J	Republica
K	Mandow Pearl
L	GTDC Tourist Hostel
M	Orav's
N	Park Lane Lodge
O	Alfonso
P	Panjim Inn
Q	GTDC Tourist Home

RESTAURANTS

1 Chunghwa
2 Sher-E-Punjab
3 Annapurna
4 Sai
5 Casa Moderna/Damodar/Fishland
6 Rosoyo
7 A Pasteleria
8 Venite
9 Vihar

SPICES

There are spice plantations scattered all over India, where you can stock up with chilli, cardamom, turmeric, ginger, cumin, nutmeg and coriander for your return journey. Alternatively, buy them at the markets.

You may be pleased to know that according to the ancient canons of Indian medicine, the myriad spices concealed in your meal are all working to improve your health. While the general combination stimulates the appetite and helps your digestion in this hot climate, some of the individual spices have some surprising properties. Turmeric is very good for skin ailments, ginger for your liver or rheumatism. Cloves help the kidneys, relieve fevers and stimulates the heart. Coriander fights constipation and insomnia. One of the most versatile is cardamom, battling bad breath, headaches, coughs and haemorrhoids.

SPRINGS

Due to Goa's peculiar topography, there are a large number of springs. Their medicinal and rejuvenating qualitites have become integrated with local folklore. Some, like the Ambora spring in Raia village, are ferruginous. The Ambora Fountain is built in the shape of a well and the water there is reputed to help the treatment of skin eruptions.

There are two springs within Aguada Fort, the lower one is believed to be effective against itches and other skin diseases.

The spring at Batim also contains iron and the water is considered a good blood purifier.

The springs such as Fonderem in Candolim and Vellin Caisua restore lost appetites. Bimbol in Sattari, Fatorpa in Bali, Raider in Cavelossim, Gango in Nachinola and Torvalem in Shiroda have light carbonic and sulphurous qualities. Springs at Curea, Merces and Boea de Vaca are known to be perennial. Other popular springs are Kesarval, Salmana in Saligao and springs in Keri, Ponda and Pomburpa.

Ponda taluka has a large number of springs emerging from the plateau. These have been judiciously collected in tanks and form the basis of traditional irrigation systems.

Chemical and microbiological tests reveal that the waters of the springs are free from contamination and are relatively clean and suitable for drinking purposes. Considerable developmental activities are essential to maintain the springs and keep their surroundings clean, since the water is often collected in tanks adjacent to the springs and is used for bathing and other domestic purposes, thereby contaminating the outflow.

SUN
The average temperature of the sun in summer is 32°C during the days and 24°C at night. During the winter too the average temperature is 32°C but at night it can drop to 22°C.

SUNBATHING
Nearly all the recognised hotels catering to foreign tourists provide sunbeds by the pool. You can even find some beachside shacks renting out a few right on the beach. Sunbathing in the nude is prohibited.

T
TAXIS
There are two kinds of taxis available on hire in Goa. The first is the yellow-topped taxi available at taxi stands and outside hotels.

Besides these regular taxis, there are also the private tourist taxis available for hire from Dabolim Airport and tourist taxi stands in major places. Most hotels have a taxi stand or can contact them for you. Some of these private taxis also have inter-state licence and can take you by road to other places in India. If you want a taxi for a morning or a day, agree on a price before you set out. The taxi will wait for you while you stop along the way.

TELEPHONE

Hotels have steep mark-ups. Phones in the street are good and much cheaper. The ISD booths charge government-approved rates so they tend to be the cheapest.

The code for the UK from Goa is: 00 44 + area code (minus the zero) + telephone number, for example: 0044 181 6281234.

TEMPLES

In the 16th century, Portuguese missionary zeal was at its most intense and Hindu priests, carrying temple deities, fled from the Old Conquests to the safety of the wooded hills of Ponda which only came under Portuguese rule in 1764. Although Goa has some 50 temples whose principal deities are refugees, not all the surviving temples were built under those conditions. Temples like the Arvalem Caves, Tambdi Surla and Chandranath survived because, like Ponda, they formed the New Conquests, that is territiories acquired in the 18th century after the Inquisition.

Goan temples with their domes with finial topknots and red-tiled sloping roofs, have a distinct architectural style. In the courtyard are lamp towers, some seven storeys high, and elaborate *vrindavans* (tulsi pots). Inside are rounded and cusped arches, a screen between the *mandapa* (hall) and inner sanctuary, carved and painted woodwork and ornate chandeliers and lamps.

Chandranath Temple, southeast of Margao, Salcete, perched on top of a hill, dating to the fifth century. The sanctuary and *linga* are carved out of the hill

Sri Chandreshwar Bhutnath Temple, Parvath, is dedicated to Shiva as the powerful Lord of the Moon. The temple is set in a clearing which had been a temple site since the fifth century or even earlier, surviving all Portuguese zeal. The short lamp towers, two temple chariots (used at festivals), the sanctuary and Nandi bull are carved from living rock

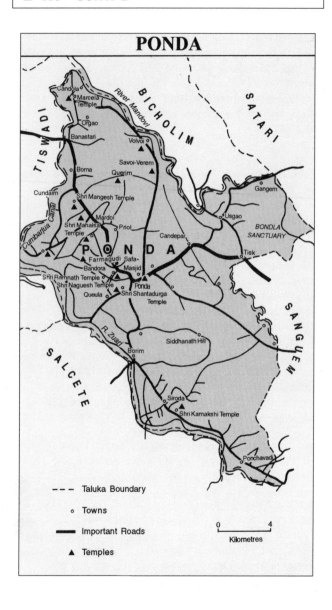

PONDA

Rock-cut Cave Temples, Arvalem, Bicholim, date to the third and sixth centuries AD and were possibly Buddhist in origin. Within are Shiva *lingas*.

Shri Bhagavati Temple, Parcem, Pernerm, is a rare temple where Brahma is worshipped. Two five-storey lamp towers flank the façade

Sri Datta Mandir, near Sanquelim Bridge, Bicholim, is a small temple, with a blue multi-tiered tower, surrounded by *peepul* and *kadamba* trees.

Sri Lakshmi Narasimha Devasthan Temple, Velinga, is Goa's most beautiful temple. The deity, Narasimha, Vishnu's fourth *avatar* (incarnation) of half-man, half-lion, was brought here by priests fleeing from Sancoale in the 1560s. The tank, set into the hillside, is fed by a spring.

Sri Mahalasa Temple, Mardol, is dedicated to Lord Vishnu. The deity was from an older temple in Mormugao taluka. In the courtyard is an impressive brass pillar set on a turtle's back and surmounted by Garuda, Vishnu's vehicle. The turtle represents Kurma, Vishnu's second *avatar* (incarnation).

Sri Mahalakshmi Temple, Bandora, was founded in the 15th century and dedicated to Lakshmi, Vishnu's consort. The deity was brought here from Colva in 1565.

Sri Mangesh Temple, Priol, is Goa's richest and most important temple, dedicated to Lord Shiva. The symbolic *linga* in the sanctum sanctorm, was rescued before the original temple in Kortalim was destroyed and brought here by ferry. The temple is built around a huge water tank, the largest in Goa. A seven-storey lamp tower stands before the main entrance to the temple.

Sri Nagesh Temple, Bandora, has an inscribed basalt slab set into the entrance stating that money was donated on 24 December 1413 for the worship of Nagesh (a form of Shiva) and Mahalakshmi. The five-storeyed lamp tower is decorated with *nagas* (snakes). A Nandi bull, Shiva's vehicle, stands outside, in front of the temple's main entrance

Sri Saptakoteshwar Temple, Naroa, Bicholim, is dedicated to the Kadambas' favourite deity. This temple was moved here from Divar Island and sponsored by the Great Maratha, Shivaji in 1668. The Shiva *linga* has rope marks as it was used by the Portuguese to draw water.

Sri Shantadurga Temple, Queula, is Goa's most popular temple built in the early 18th century

Tambdi Surla Temple, beyond Sancordem, Sanguem, is one of Goa's oldest temples dating to the 13th century. The small, beautifully carved and perfectly proportioned black basalt temple, dedicated to Lord Shiva, is reminiscent of Aihole's temples in neighbouring Karnataka

TIME
Time difference: Indian Standard Time (IST) is GMT plus five and a half hours.

	Goa	London
end-October to end-March	12.00 noon	06.30 am
end-March to end-October	12.00 noon	07.30 am

TIPPING
It is customary to tip about ten percent in restaurants. Elsewhere, tipping is discouraged by the government of India. Do not try to tip government employees, although museum guides will invariably give hints at the end of a conducted tour. In temples, a token donation of Rs5 to 10 is more or less mandatory; you should also give a

couple of rupees to the person who looked after your
shoes while you were visiting.

TOUR OPERATORS
Journeys Tours and Travels (I) Private Limited (IATA
Oriented), Mathias Plaza, Second Floor, 18th June Road,
Panaji, tel: 223232
Konkan Tours and Travels, 31 January Road, Panaji,
tel: 458774
Sita World Travels Private Limited, Rizvi Chambers,
C Albuquerque Road, Panaji, tel: 22141814
Trans Goa Tours and Travels, G 11 Shankar Parvati
Building, 18th June Road, Opposite Education Department,
Panaji, tel: 460906
Velho Travels, Below Miranda Hospital, Margao, tel: 221968

TOURIST INFORMATION
The Government of Goa's Department of Tourism supplies
basic maps and information and can give useful local tips.
Their offices are at:
Department of Tourism Office, near Patto Bridge, Panaji
Tourist Information Centre, Municipal Building, Margao
Tourist Information Centre, near Railway Station, Vasco
Tourist Information Centre, Dabolim Airport, Dabolim
Tourist Information Centre, Kadamba Bus Stand, Panaji

For information on other parts of India, try:
Government of India Tourist Officer, Church Square, Panaji
Maharashtra Tourist Information Bureau, Tourist Hostel,
Panaji
Karnataka Tourist Information Centre, Velhos Building,
Municipal Garden Square, Panaji
Andhra Pradesh Tourist Information, Rua de Qurem, Panaji
Tamil Nadu Tourist Information Office, T Raju Chambers,
Dr A B Road, Panaji

TOWNS

Mapusa

Mapusa is the capital of Bardez taluka and North Goa's major town. It is most famous for its weekly Friday Market, where traders from all the neighbouring areas come to trade in everything from spices to livestock (also see MARKETS).

The church of Mapusa is St Jerome's, but the main altar of the church is dedicated to Our Lady of Miracles, who is held in great veneration by both Hindus and Catholics.

Mapusa's important temples are Maruti in the town centre and Bogdeshwar, recently built in the paddy fields between the Panaji-Mapusa and the Parra-Calangute roads.

Margao

Goa's second largest city is capital of Salcete taluka (district) and the commercial centre of South Goa. It is the only town besides Panaji of any architectural distinction. Margao's Church of the Holy Spirit is one of Goa's most magnificient, overlooking a square lined with lavish houses. The annual church feast (last Sunday of May) is when locals buy their monsoon store of dry fish, prawns and onions (also see MARKETS). On the hill above the city stands the Nossa Senhora de Piedade chapel, built in 1820.

Margao's history can be traced back to the Pandava Caves at Aquem Alto, next to the Chapel of Saint Sebastian.

The city is linked by railway with Mormugao, Ponda and the rest of India.

Some of Goa's finest old mansions are concentrated in and around Margao. For those who whould like to see some of the greatest houses, **Classical Interlude** (Casa dos Mirandos, Loutulim, tel: 277022 or G 2 La Marvel, Dona Paula, tel: 222176) arranges tours which add another dimension to the Goa experience.

Good private operators include:
Barracuda Diving, Vainguinim Beach, tel: 403004/221133
Goa Diving, Bogmalo Beach, tel: 514997
Hydro-Sports Goa, Vainguinim Beach, Dona Paula, tel: 221133
Water Sports Goa, Bogmalo Beach, tel: 514997

Finally, **Mermaid Boating Club** hires out up to four single-seater fibreglass kayaks to those brave enough to try out Goa's coastal waters. The club is being managed by Mr Philip Vaz who can be reached by telephone (277439) or at his residence at Salmona.

WILDLIFE SANCTUARIES
Bhagwan Mahavir Wildlife Sanctuary
Situated along the northeastern border of Goa, at Molem, about an hour and a half's journey fron Panaji, this sanctuary covers 240 square kilometres of the dense forest-clad slopes of the Western Ghats. Believed to be the state's largest sanctuaries, it is rich in wildlife, and is also a birdwatcher's paradise. It is common to see stampeding sambar, grazing chitals, langurs, wild boar and barking deer. From here, the Dudhsagar Falls is an hour's journey by train.

Bondla Forest Sanctuary
This sanctuary, in Ponda taluka, is eight square kilometres in area, and 52 kilometres from Panaji. It is really a small zoo, deer park and botanical garden. For garden–lovers, various plants are available on sale here. The zoo and gardens are closed on Thursdays.

Cotigao Wildlife Sanctuary
Covering 105 square kilometres, this sanctuary is located in Canacona at the southern tip of Goa, about 60 kilometres from Panaji. The land is part hills, part plains and is covered with dense forest and is well known for its varied wildlife (flora and fauna and reptiles). The ancient Jeevottam Partagal Math, noted for Vedic studies, lies within.

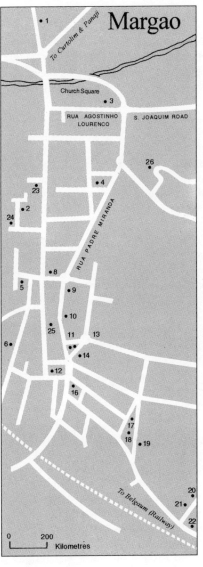

1   Kadamba Bus Station
2   Twiga Lodge
3   Margao Church
4   Hotel Metropole
5   Poste Restante
6   Goa Woodlands
7   Bank
8   GPO
9   Mabai Hotel
10 Marliz
11 Kandeel Restaurant
12 Tourist Office & Bar & Kamat
    Hotel
13 Buses to Colva
14 La Marina
15 Market
16 Rukrish Hotel
17 Paradise Bar and Restaurant
18 Centaur Lodging
19 Milan Kamat Hotel
20 Vishranti Lodge
21 Sangram Boarding
22 Hotel Sanrit
23 Damodar Temple
24 Vitoba Mandir
25 Jorge Barreto Park
26 Hospital

Panaji

Panaji is the capital of Goa. The name is derived from a mixture of Portuguese and Konkani and means 'land that can never get flooded', which is a fact. When Old Goa was the capital of Goa, Panaji was inhabited only by fishermen. The then Muslim ruler Yusuf Ali Adil Shah had his holiday palace here, which today houses the Secretariat of Goa.

Panaji lies on the banks of the River Mandovi. Its government buildings built in the modern and neo-Classical style have altered the town's colonial appearance. Opposite the Secretariat is the statue of Abbé de Faria (1756-1819), a Goan priest from Candolim who was a Professor of Philosophy at Marseilles University. It was he who introduced hypnotism to the Western world during the French Revolution.

The majestic Church of the Immaculate Conception overlooks the commercial centre of Panaji.

Diagonally to the Church Square is Dada Vaidya Road where the Jama Masjid Mosque, Mahalakshmi Temple (1818) and Cabeca de Vaca (now Boca de Vaca) Fountain are all found.

Behind all this is the hilltop called Altinho, a posh residential area. The Palace of the Archbishop is here and the All India Radio (AIR) studios, the Lyceum buildings and the Serra Home for the Aged.

Fontainhas is the oldest residential area of Panaji. Its name derives from a fountain at the foot of the Maruti Temple (dedicated to the Hindu god Hanuman) situated there. The narrow winding streets and quaint houses are strongly Portuguese with their railed and balustraded balconies and the ornamental roof canopies.

Campal lies along the riverside boulevard leading eastwards out of town. The Goa Kala Academy (Art Academy) is here, the state's foremost institution for the promotion of art and culture. Campal also has a football stadium of 5,000 capacity, a cricket stadium, an Olympic size swimming pool and a basket–ball court. Beyond lies Miramar, the closest beach to Panaji.

Ponda

Ponda, capital of Ponda taluka, has a strategic position between Panaji, Margao, and Bicholim. Within a span of three to five kilometres of the city, can be found the impressive temples built by Hindus fleeing Portuguese persecution. Good churches include Santa Anna (1700) and Chapel of Our Lady of Carmo (1782).

Vasco da Gama

Vasco da Gama is Goa's port town and capital of Mormugao taluka. It lies on the southern bank of the River Zuari and is connected to Mormugao Harbour by an isthmus.

In the late 1600s (1681-1686) the Portuguese chose Mormugao to replace Old Goa (capital of Goa), under constant threat of attack from the Muslims, Marathas and the plague. Several buildings were constructed near the harbour. Then Lisbon ordered that the capital be shifted to Panaji instead.

Today's city grew around the fort and the port.

TRANSPORT

Travel in Goa can be undertaken in several ways. The easiest one being hiring a tourist taxi. Goa has a bus service, a rail service, ferry service and taxis, both the two-wheeler and the four-wheeler variety.

For more details see BUSES, FERRIES, RAILWAYS, TAXIS.

TRAVEL AGENCIES

Panaji

MGM International Travels, Mamai Camotim Building, near V P Sinari, tel: 225150

Raj Travel and Tours Limited, Opposite Azad Maidan, Rua de Ormuz, tel: 224980

Rauraje Deshprabhu, Rua Cunha Riviera, Panaji, tel: 221840

Sarken Tour Operators, Panaji, tel: 46828

Trade Wings Limited, A-6 Mascarenhas Building, M G Road, Panaji, tel: 42430

Margao
Dynamic Tours and Travels, Lourenco Apartments, tel:720197, 723586
St Alex Travels, tel:720452

Mapusa
Pink Panther Travel Agency, Coscar Building, Taliwada, tel: 263180
U K Travels, Chandranath Apartments, Opposite Police Station, tel: 263037

V

VISA
All overseas travellers entering India need a valid visa.

VOLTAGE
Voltage fluctuations are very frequent in Goa. So it is essential to check the voltage before using any electrical appliances. The voltage is usually 220 volts AC, 50 cycles.

W

WATER
It is advisable not to drink tap water in India. Bottled water is available in most shops, bars and restaurants. To avoid 'Delhi Belly', use bottled water even when brushing your teeth and do not take ice cubes in your drinks.

WATER SPORTS
Water sports have only recently been introduced to Goa. Several hotels and private operators now offer fishing, sailing, para-sailing, water-skiing, wind surfing, diving, water scooters, boat rides and river cruises.

The Taj Group of Hotels has a good range of facilities as does Cidade de Goa. Most four- and five-star hotels offer some water sports. At the Dona Paula Bay, one can hire water scooters and go on boat rides.